CREATIVE
CROCHET
Projects

Creative Crochet Projects

Landauer Publishing, www.landauerpub.com, is an imprint of Fox Chapel Publishing Company, Inc.

Project Team

Editor: Hayley DeBerard

Cover Designer: David Fisk

Layout Designer: Llara Pazdan

Indexer: Nancy Arndt

Photo Credits: Photography by Stephanie Pokorny unless otherwise noted; dim_as_333: crochet hooks, pg 9; Brixel: pom-pom maker, pg 38; Fox Chapel Design Team: cover, back cover, title page, pgs 5, 29, 37, 42, 45, 50, 51, 53, 57, 59, 60, 63, 67, 68, 71, 73, 76, 79, 81, 82, 85, 87, 89, 90, 93; Hayley DeBerard: crochet stitches, pgs 14-17.

Additional credits: Graphic elements used throughout: Elena Eskevich, Rudenko Roman, Yevgenij_D, Sakarin Sawasdinaka, and W. Phokin / Shutterstock.com; Sentimental postman / CreativeMarket.com.

ISBN 978-1-947163-63-8

The Cataloging-in-Publication Data is on file with the Library of Congress.

We are always looking for talented authors. To submit an idea, please send a brief inquiry to acquisitions@foxchapelpublishing.com.

Printed in Singapore

23 22 21 20   2 4 6 8 10 9 7 5 3 1

12 PLAYFUL PROJECTS
for Beginners and Beyond

Stephanie Pokorny

CONTENTS

INTRODUCTION 6

FUN ACCESSORIES TO MAKE AND WEAR 18

Finger Crochet Scarves

20

It's a Cinch One-Hour Cowl

26

Squiggles McGee Hat

30

Bubble Hue Shift Hat

34

Asymmetric Owl Wrap

40

PLAYTIME PROJECTS 50

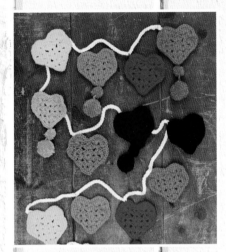

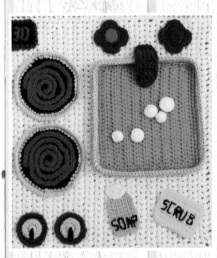

INTRODUCTION

Hi! Hello! Welcome to *Creative Crochet Projects*!

Come on in, pick up your hook, and stay a while. I am so glad you are here.

I have always been a "maker" in some form or another for as long as I can remember. While most children were asking to go to the toy store, my grandma and grandpa were always met with pleas for trips to the craft store. Creating was my ideal playtime.

Growing up, my mom was always making things, from home décor to my costumes for Halloween. DIY'ers have surrounded me my whole life. Thank goodness because it led me here to this book and to you! Crochet is my absolute passion. It offers unlimited possibilities for creating, from afghans that keep your loved ones toasty warm to extreme structural costumes and pieces. As a mother of four boys, my children are my driving force in creating. There is not much better than having your kids come and ask, "Momma, can you make me...?" and you are able to oblige. Handmade is a treasure to me!

Within this book you will find creative projects for every level of crocheter: from absolute beginner, to more advanced projects, and plenty in between. Have fun filling your child's play kitchen with plush toys like the Sliceable Watermelon, Roll-Away Kitchen Playmat, or the customizable Foldable Hamburger. Or make some colorful accessories that are just as fun to make as they are to wear such as the fun Finger Crochet Scarves, the Squiggles McGee Hat, or a personal favorite, the Asymmetric Owl Wrap. I hope all the patterns within this book inspire you to "play" with your crochet.

I welcome you to follow me on social media @Crochetverse to share your projects from the book.

Much Love and Yarn,

Stephanie Pokorny

GET READY TO START

Understanding a Crochet Pattern

If you're new to crochet, this chapter will walk you through some of the basic materials, tools, terminology, and techniques that will help you understand a crochet pattern and get you crocheting in no time. I've also included a quick lesson on how to measure for accurate pattern gauge that will help take your projects to the next level!

Yarn Weight and Fiber Content

The first part of starting any crochet pattern is deciding what yarn to use and how much of it is needed. Luckily, it's pretty easy to figure out as most patterns will list off the suggested weight, brand, color, and amount of yarn needed to complete the project as shown. For best results, you will want to choose the same yarn or something you know to be quite similar to the suggested yarn. If you are unfamiliar with the yarn, the people at your local craft stores and independent yarn shops are a great source for knowledge on this subject! Yarn weights can feel daunting to understand, but the system is not overly difficult once you become familiar with it. Yarn is given three denotations that help you understand its weight: a word description, a numerical weight, and a "ply" count. The word description and numerical weight are typically how the United States describes yarn. Ply count is most often used outside the U.S. This is not a steadfast rule, but a basic generalization of what you will encounter. Using the chart on page 9, we can summarize, for example, that medium weight, or worsted weight yarn is the same as #4 yarn and 10–12 ply yarn.

At times, a pattern will instruct you to work "holding the yarn double stranded." This simply means that you will lay two strands of yarn next to each other (from different skeins or balls) and work the pattern as directed, holding the two strands as one. This is often done to achieve a stiffer finished project where structure is important to the final piece.

Keep in mind that different fiber compositions behave differently in finished items. Therefore, you will want to choose a yarn with the same or similar composition as the recommended yarn. Yarn has many compositions. Acrylic yarns are a great place to start, as they are soft, affordable, and last quite long through machine washings. Cotton yarns can be stiffer but produce items that are breathable and good for warmer weather. Natural fibers such as wool, alpaca, and angora can be pricey but create heirloom quality garments that feel luxurious. Note that even though two yarns may be marked as medium/worsted/#4 on the label, true weight can vary greatly amongst different manufacturers. This is why checking gauge every time is of utmost importance. This will be discussed later in this section.

Crochet Hooks

The pattern instructions will also state the hook size the pattern designer used when making the project. Each crochet hook is marked with a size in millimeters (mm) and, depending on the size, a coordinating letter size. Sometimes, a pattern uses multiple hook sizes. Select the stated hook size to begin but keep in mind that hook sizes are a recommendation or "starting point."

Yarn Weight	Numerical Weight	Type of Yarns in Category	Ply Count
Lace	0	Fingering 10-count crochet thread	1–2
Super Fine	1	Sock, Fingering, Baby	3–4
Fine	2	Sport, Baby	5
Light	3	DK, Light Worsted	8
Medium	4	Worsted, Afghan, Aran	10–12
Bulky	5	Chunky, Craft, Rug	14
Super Bulky	6	Super Bulky, Roving	16
Jumbo	7	Jumbo, Roving	16 and up

Crochet Hook Sizes

US Hook Symbol	Millimeter Size
B/1	2–2.25 mm
C/2	2.75 mm
D/3	3.25 mm
E/4	3.5 mm
F/5	3.75 mm
G/6	4–4.25 mm
7	4.5 mm
H/8	5 mm
I/9	5.5 mm
J/10	6 mm
K/10½	6.5 mm
L/11	8 mm
M/13	9 mm
N/15	10 mm
P/16	12 mm
Q	15 mm
S	20 mm

Gauge

Gauge is a measurement system that counts the number of stitches and rows in a specific-sized swatch of crocheted material. It allows you to compare your tension to the tension of the person who designed the pattern. This is important because we all crochet with varying degrees of tension. You may find that by using the recommended hook size in a pattern your stitches are too loose or too tight when compared to the written gauge. This will require you to adjust your hook size, so your resulting swatch is the same as the pattern suggests. Many things affect gauge including hook choice, yarn choice, and personal technique. To ensure that your finished project results are the same as the project pictured, you must be sure your tension is the same as the pattern states. It is particularly important for anything that will be worn as a garment or accessory, as the fit will be affected if your gauge is off. Gauge may seem slightly less important on items where size doesn't need to be precise, such as afghans or home decor. However, you'll want to stick close to the suggested gauge still, as working looser puts you at risk of running out of supplies.

Let's discuss two examples of how gauge may be listed in a pattern.

Basic Swatch

To make a basic crochet gauge swatch, use the recommended hook size and yarn weight to crochet a square of fabric in the suggested stitch. The pattern will outline the width and height of an ideal swatch, measured across the indicated number of stitches and rows. For example: *14 sts by 9 rows in half double crochet = 4" x 4" using worsted weight yarn and Size US H (5 mm) crochet hook.* How do we check this? Begin by chaining slightly larger than the recommended 4" using the hook and the yarn you plan to use for the project. You can always measure within the swatch if your created piece ends up larger than the suggested size. Work across the beginning chain in the stitch stated, in this case half double crochet. Work the number of rows stated in the swatch. Lay your resulting piece on a flat surface, making sure it is smooth but not stretched. In the image, we see that in the 4" width there are 14 stitches and in the 4" height there are 9 rows. This means gauge has been matched and we can proceed onto the actual project. What if your count is not the same? If you have *more* stitches and rows than stated, your tension/gauge is *looser* than the pattern. *Drop a hook size* and try the swatch again. If you have *fewer* stitches and rows than stated, your tension/gauge is *tighter* than the pattern. *Go up* a hook size and try the swatch again.

Gauge as Part of Pattern

Gauge can also be tested as part of the pattern. This is what you will most often find in this book and my preferred way to check gauge to be most accurate. As an example, a gauge check will state: *Rnds 1-3 of pattern equals 3" in diameter.* To test this, use the recommended hook size and yarn you plan to use for the project and work the specified number of rounds. Once completed, you will then measure. Note that in the image to the right, gauge has been met, as three rounds of crochet measures 3" in diameter. As with the basic swatch method, larger dimensions mean your tension is looser and you'll need to drop a hook size. Opposingly, smaller dimensions mean your tension is tighter and you'll need to go up a hook size.

With the basic method for measuring gauge, create a swatch as indicated in the pattern. In this example the pattern called for 9 rows and 14 stitches to equal 4"x4" to match gauge.

4"

4"

When checking gauge as part of the pattern, begin working as directed, then stop and measure when indicated. In this example, the pattern called for the project to measure 3" in diameter after completing 3 rounds.

3"

Basic Crochet Tool Kit

Each pattern in this book lists a basic tool kit as a necessary item in the notions section. This includes four general tools that you need to have on hand.

- A **tapestry needle** is a larger, blunt-tipped needle with an oversized eye or top opening that you can use to weave yarn ends in to secure them. There are many different kinds available; from plastic to metal, to ones bent at the tip. When weaving in your ends, you will want to sew the yarn up, then down, working through the body of nearby stitches. Then weave across 2-3 stitches horizontally along the rows. Weaving in multiple directions and within the plies of yarn in the stitches will ensure the ends will stay tight and not unravel as the item is used.

- A sharp pair of **scissors** is needed to trim up ends and cut yarns for color changes or when finishing a piece.

- A **ruler** or **measuring tape** allows you to check gauge or measurements in the pattern for fit. A rigid ruler is best for measuring gauge or crocheted pieces; while a soft measuring tape is preferred for measuring parts of the body to select sizing when needed.

- **Stitch markers** are used to mark a stitch in the pattern for placement or keeping track of counts in rounds or rows completed. There are a very wide range of styles available from split ring to locking. Some crocheters simply use scrap pieces of yarn within the stitch to mark and then pull the scrap out later once completed. Even basic bobby pins make nice stitch markers! Feel free to get creative!

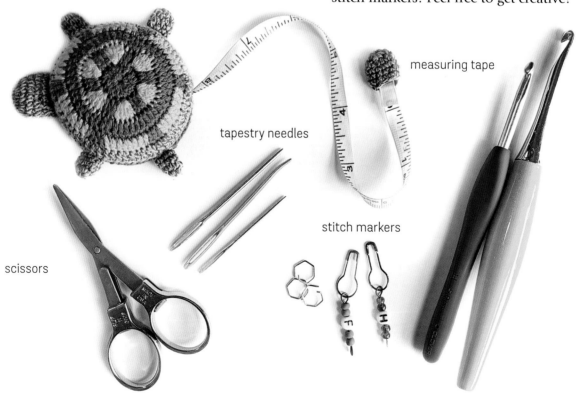

measuring tape

tapestry needles

stitch markers

scissors

The notions needed to make a beautiful finished crochet project aren't fancy. The basics include the items shown here. Add a notions pouch to hold them all and you're ready to take your crochet on the road!

Abbreviations and Basic Stitches

Abbreviations

This book is written in U.S. terms and uses standard abbreviations for crochet. The method allows us to write patterns to be universally understood with ease. Refer to the alphabetical list shown if you find you are unfamiliar with a certain abbreviation you encounter while working.

bb	back bump		**lp**	loop
bp	back post		**rem**	remain; remaining
beg	begin; beginning		**rep**	repeat; repeating
bet	between		**revsc**	reverse single crochet
blo	back loop only		**rnd**	round
ch	chain		**sc**	single crochet
cl	cluster		**sk**	skip
cont	continue; continuing		**sl**	slip
dc	double crochet		**sp**	space
dec	decrease; decreasing; decreased		**st**	stitch
flo	front loop only		**tog**	together
fp	front post		**tr**	treble crochet
hdc	half double crochet		**yo**	yarn over

Basic Crochet Stitches

Crochet is very simple, as it basically consists of just a few different stitches, all of which are worked in a very similar way—it is their heights that vary. There is only ever one stitch on the hook at any one time, and the new stitches are worked by inserting the hook through the work, wrapping the yarn around the hook, and pulling these loops of yarn through the stitch on the hook. In addition, some patterns may use what is called a "special stitch." These may be unique or less common stitches, or a stitch created specifically for that project.

Slipknot

Almost all crochet projects start with a slipknot. With crochet, there is only ever one stitch on the hook at any time and the slipknot is the starting point for all the stitches that go to make up the finished work.

When you make a slipknot, ensure the cut end of yarn is the end you need to pull to tighten the loop. Slip this loop over the crochet hook and pull up the end so the loop sits comfortably around the crochet hook, just below the actual hook section (Fig. 1). The resulting loop on your hook is your first stitch.

Chain

Almost all crochet will begin with a long chain of simple stitches that are used as the foundation for the rest of the work. These stitches are called "chain" stitches and the starting string is called the "foundation chain."

Wrap the yarn around the hook, bringing it up from the back, over the hook, and taking it back to the back below the hook—this is called yarning over. Now gently pull this loop of yarn through the loop already on the hook. Continue wrapping the yarn over the hook and drawing new stitches through until you have the required number of chain stitches (Fig. 2). It is quite easy to count the stitches—along the chain there will be one neat "V" for each chain stitch.

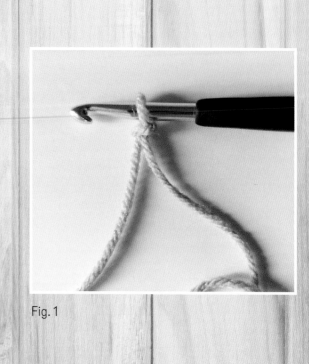

Fig. 1

Fig. 2

Fig. 3

Fig. 4

Fig. 5

Fig. 6

Slip Stitch

This is the smallest of all stitches, as it adds no height to the work, and is usually used to join two pieces or to move the hook to a new starting point.

Insert the hook into the specified place, yarn over and draw this loop through both the stitch the hook was inserted through and the working loop (Fig. 3).

Single Crochet

This is one of the most common stitches you'll run across in crochet patterns and is used often throughout this book. Because of its short height, single crochet creates a denser fabric than other stitches.

Insert your hook into the next stitch, yarn over, and draw up a loop (Fig. 4). Yarn over again and draw it through both loops on hook.

Reverse Single Crochet

A simple variation of single crochet most often used for edging, reverse single crochet is sometimes called crab stitch because of its "backward" motion.

Working from left to right, insert hook in next stitch to right, draw the yarn around hook, and pull this loop through the stitches. Yarn over again and pull through both loops on hook (Fig. 5).

Half Double Crochet

As its name implies, this stitch falls in height between a single crochet and a double crochet. It produces a fairly tight fabric similar to one made with single crochet stitch.

Yarn over, then, insert hook in stitch. Yarn over again and pull up loop—there are now three loops on the hook (Fig. 6). Yarn over one last time and draw through all loops on hook.

Double Crochet

This is a slightly taller stitch, is frequently used for edgings, and is one of the most well-known crochet stitches.

Yarn over and insert hook into work, draw up a loop. There are now three loops on the hook. Yarn over again and draw through the first two loops on the hook (Fig. 7). Yarn over and pull through the remaining two loops on the hook.

Fig. 7

Treble Crochet

Treble crochet, or sometimes called triple crochet, can be used both for simple and complicated stitch patterns that call for more height than double crochet.

Yarn over twice and insert the hook into the work. Yarn over again and draw the yarn through the new loop. There will be four loops on the hook. (Fig. 8)

Yarn over again and draw through first two loops. Yarn over and draw through the next two loops (Fig. 9). Make one final yarn over again, pull through the two remaining loops on the hook.

Fig. 8

Fig. 9

Fig. 10

Fig. 11

Fig. 12

Fig. 13

Color Change

Sometimes patterns call for you to switch from one colored yarn to another using a color change. For example, a pattern might say, "Change to B, cut A" to indicate changing from the main color yarn to the accent color.

Work stitch as normal until final yarn over (Fig. 10). Instead of finishing the stitch with the previous color, make the final yarn over with the new colored yarn. In this case, the last yarn over in a double crochet is made using a new colored yarn.

Continue working in new color yarn (Fig. 11). Only cut the previous colored yarn if specified.

Magic Ring

This easy technique allows you to create an adjustable loop to start circular projects without there being a big hole in the middle.

Start by making a large loop with the yarn. Holding the loop with your fingers, insert hook into loop and pull working yarn through loop (Fig. 12).

Continue to work indicated number of stitches into loop. Pull on yarn tail tight to close loop (Fig. 13).

FUN ACCESSORIES
to Make and Wear

In this chapter, you will find a colorful assortment of crocheted accessories that are fun and exciting enough to make again and again. I encourage you to use these patterns as jumping off points that you can use to play with color and style to make customized designs that are uniquely you!

34

20

26

30

40

FINGER CROCHET
Scarves

No hooks are needed to make these playful scarves, just your fingers, making this the perfect place to start for beginners or those looking to introduce crochet to kids.

I've included a quick lesson on how to finger crochet to get you started, but you'll be amazed at just how quickly you'll get the hang of this fun technique. Test out your new skills by making either the Stately Stranded (solid color) or Braided Beauty (multi color) finger scarf patterns included or use them as inspiration to dream up your own finger crochet projects!

FINISHED SIZE

Scarves measure approximately 5' long.

YARN

Super Bulky weight (#6 Super Bulky).

Stately Stranded: Knit Picks Tuff Puff (100% wool; 44 yards/100 grams): Celestial, 4 skeins.

Braided Beauty: Knit Picks Tuff Puff (100% wool; 44 yards/100 grams): Jelly, Chartreuse, Silver, 2 skeins each.

NOTIONS

Basic crochet tool kit.

Pom-pom maker or method of choice to create 4.5" pom-pom (*I used an Extra Large [4.5"] Clover Pom-Pom Maker*).

GAUGE

While gauge is not of critical importance, try to keep an even tension and lp height of 2" throughout to achieve proper drape and ensure the same quantity of yarn is used. We will be measuring the completed strands as opposed to counting the chains.

Braided Beauty Scarf

STATELY STRANDED SCARF

1 Holding the yarn double stranded the entire work: Leave a 10" long beg and end tail for assembly later. Using the *"How to Finger Crochet"* lesson on page 25, and keeping an approximate 2" lp size, finger crochet six strands that are 5 ft long each. When you measure, be sure not to stretch the strand. Just lay it flat and measure. Do not pull the last lp tightly yet. This will allow you to remove chs as needed so all final ch strands are the same length. Once all six strands are done, match all the beg sl lps tog and make sure the strands are the same length. Remove chs as needed, then pull the end tail through the last lp tightly to secure and trim end to a 10" length.

2 Lay all the strands next to each other, matching all the beg sl lps tog on one end and all the final chains tog on the opposite end. Using a standard overhand knot and holding all the tails as one; knot one end tog, then rep for the other end.

3 Now, take all the tails and using a tapestry needle, weave them back up into the strands on both ends of the scarf. You will now have a long scarf with two knotted ends.

4 Create two 4½" pom-poms using your preferred method. Using the tails from the pom-pom, snuggle the knot of one end of the scarf inside a pom-pom so it's cohesive and the knot is mostly hidden, and weave tails up into the scarf. Rep for the other side.

BRAIDED BEAUTY SCARF

1 Holding the yarn double stranded for the entire work: Using the *"How to Finger Crochet"* lesson, and keeping an approximate 2" lp size, finger crochet three strands in each of the three colors that are 6 ft long. When you measure, be sure not to stretch the strand, just lay it flat and measure. Keep your beg and end tails about 10" long each so they can be knotted tog easily. You will have nine total strands, three each of three colors.

2 Now, using a standard overhand knot, line up three strands, one of each color. Holding all the tails as one, knot these three tog on one end. I stuck the knot inside a drawer and closed it so it would be held firmly to proceed. You could also have someone hold it for you. Braid these three strands tog in a standard braid to the opposite end. Overhand knot the tails tog to secure just like you did in the beg.

3 Rep step 2 twice more. You now have three braided strands. Using the tail ends, line up the beg knot from each strand. Using the tails or a separate piece of yarn, sew the three braids tog at one end. Weave all ends rem into the braided strands. Rep for the opposite end.

4 Create two 6" pom-poms using your preferred method. Snuggle the knot of the end of the scarf inside the pom-pom so it's cohesive and use the tails from the pom-pom to secure. Weave the tails up into the scarf. Rep for the other side.

How to Finger Crochet

1 Leaving a 10" tail, lp the yarn so the working end (end attached to the yarn ball) is on top.

2 Dive your pointer finger and thumb in the center of the lp and pull up the working end through the lp made first.

3 Pull both the tail and working end to tighten the slipknot, so the lp measures 2" tall.

4 In the same manner, dive your fingers in the center of the lp just made, grab the working yarn and again pull up a lp about 2". Measure them until you get a feel for how that looks; then just estimate.

5 Rep step 4 until desired ch length is reached. Once done, trim the working yarn leaving an 10" tail and pull through the final lp. Tug tightly to secure.

IT'S A CINCH
One-Hour Cowl

Using super-bulky yarn and a large hook, this cowl works up extremely fast making it a real cinch!

Perfect for gift giving or craft fairs, you're sure to find yourself making this pattern again and again. Play with different color combinations to create a look as unique as you are!

FINISHED SIZE

Cowl measures approximately 11.5" tall x 34" circumference.

YARN

Bulky weight (#5 Bulky).

Pink Version: Madelinetosh Home (100% Merino wool; 110 yards): Neon Peach (A), 1 skein.

Madelinetosh A.S.A.P (100% Merino wool; 90 yards): Charcoal (B), 1 skein.

Green Version: Lion Brand Wool-Ease Thick & Quick (80% Acrylic, 20% Wool; 106 yards/170 grams): #612 Coney Island (A), #178 Cilantro (B), 1 skein each.

HOOK

Size US P (12 mm) crochet hook.

Adjust hook size as necessary to obtain correct gauge.

NOTIONS

Basic crochet tool kit.

GAUGE

While not imperative, to maintain yarn amounts stated, the first two rows as written should measure about 2" tall and 34" long.

Pink Version

COWL

With A, ch 62.

Row 1: Hdc in 2nd ch from hook (sk ch does not count as a st), hdc in each rem ch across. (61 hdc)

Row 2: Ch 1 (does not count as a st here and throughout), turn, hdc in same st as ch-1, *ch 1, sk next st, hdc in next st, rep from * to the end of the row.

Row 3: Ch 1, turn, hdc in each st and in each ch-1 sp across.

Rows 4-5: Rep Rows 2-3, changing to B at final yo of last st of Row 5, cut A.

Row 6: Ch 1, turn, hdcblo in each st across. (61 hdcblo)

Rows 7-10: Rep Rows 2-3, twice more, at end of Row 10, change to A at final yo of last st, cut B.

Row 11: Ch 1, turn, hdcflo in each st across.

Rows 12-15: Rep Rows 2-3, twice more, at end of Row 15, cut yarn leaving long tail for sewing.

FINISHING

Sew Ends Tog

Using the end tail from Row 15, sew the two short ends tog. It does not have to be perfect; it will be covered by the Cinch Band. Weave in all ends.

Cinch Band

With B, ch 18.

Row 1: Sc in 2nd ch from hook and each rem ch across. (17 sc)

Row 2: Ch 1, turn, sc in each st across. (17 sc)

Rows 3-7: Rep Row 2, after Row 7, cut yarn leaving long tail for sewing.

Sew Cinch Band On

Making sure the ridged side (the textured side created by the front lp and back lp sts) of cowl is facing out, wrap the cinch band around the cowl over the seam made from sewing ends tog. Sew the short ends of cinch band tog around the main cowl, encircling it. Arrange the cowl at the cinched portion to your liking, then secure the band in place with a few sts through all the layers making sure the seamed ends of the cinch band are on the inside (smooth side) of cowl. Weave in any rem ends.

Green Version

SQUIGGLES MCGEE
Hat

Offered in three sizes, make this spunky hat for the whole family! A simple tube construction gathered at the end creates a unique hat that is easy to make and sure to stand out.

FINISHED SIZES

Hat circumference measures approximately 18", 20", 21".

TO FIT: Toddler, Youth, Adult.

YARN

Worsted weight (#4 Medium).

Shown here: Knit Picks Mighty Stitch (80% acrylic, 20% wool; 208 yards/100 grams): Gulfstream (A), Serrano (B), White (C), 1 skein each.

HOOK

Size US H (5 mm) crochet hook.

Adjust hook size as necessary to obtain correct gauge.

NOTIONS

Basic crochet tool kit.

GAUGE

Check after Rnd 1, information given within pattern.

NOTES

- This hat is worked from brim to crown: starting with a ribbed band, and working up into the body of the hat, changing color strategically to showcase the squiggly design.

- St counts are given as (Toddler, Youth, Adult). Follow the count that is in the position for the size you are making.

- Do not turn rnds.

- Place a marker in the first or last st of each round to keep track.

- During color changes, do not cut the previous colored yarn unless specified. Instead, carry the yarns you are not currently using up inside the hat loosely to minimize ends to weave in.

HAT

With A, ch (72, 80, 88) sl st to first st made to form a ring.

Rnd 1: Ch 1 (does not count as a st here and throughout), hdc in same ch and in each rem ch around, sl st to first hdc made. (72, 80, 88 hdc)

GAUGE CHECK: Lay Rnd 1 doubled and flattened but not stretched. It should measure about 9" x ½" for toddler size, 10" x ½" for youth size, and 10½" x ½" for adult size.

Rnd 2: Ch 1, hdcfp in same st as ch-1, hdcfp in next st, hdcbp in next 2 sts, *hdcfp in next 2 sts, hdcbp in next 2 sts, rep from * around, sl st to the top of first hdcfp made.

Rnd 3: Ch 1, hdcfp in each hdcfp and hdcbp in each hdcbp around, sl st to top of first hdcfp.

Rnd 4: Rep Rnd 3.

Rnd 5: Follow the instruction for your chosen size only.

Toddler ONLY: Ch 1, sc in same st as ch-1 and in each st around, sl st to first sc made. (72 sc)

Youth ONLY: Ch 1, 2 sc in same st as ch-1, sc in each rem st around, sl st to first sc made. (81 sc)

Adult ONLY: Ch 1, 2 sc in the same st as ch-1, 2 sc in next st, sc in each rem st around, sl st to first sc made. (90 sc)

Rnd 6: Ch 1 (does not count as a st here and throughout), hdcblo in first 4 sts (beg in the same st the ch-1 emerges from), ch 2, sk next st, *hdcblo in next 8 sts, ch 2, sk next st, rep from * until 4 sts rem, hdcblo in last 4 sts, sl st to first hdcblo made. (Toddler: 64 hdc, and 8 ch-2 sps, Youth: 72 hdc, and 9 ch-2 sps, Adult: 80 hdc, and 10 ch-2 sps)

Note: St counts will remain the same for each round. To count subsequent rnds, refer to the counts at the end of Rnd 6.

Rnd 7: Ch 1, hdcdec over first 2 sts, hdc in next 2 sts, (hdc, ch 2, hdc) all in the next ch-2 sp, *hdc in next 2 sts (take care the first one is hidden), (hdcdec over next 2 sts) twice, hdc in next 2 sts, (hdc, ch 2, hdc) all in the next ch-2 sp, rep from * until 4 sts rem, hdc in next 2 sts, hdcdec over last 2 sts, sl st to first hdcdec made, change to B. Cut A.

Rnd 8: Ch 1, hdcblodec over the first 2 sts (the one the ch-1 emerges from and the next), hdcblo in the next 2 sts, (hdc, ch 2, hdc) all in next ch-2 sp,* hdcblo in the next 2 sts, (hdcblo dec over the next 2 sts) twice, hdcblo in the next 2 sts, (hdc, ch 2, hdc) all in next ch-2 sp, rep from *, until 4 sts rem, hdcblo in the next 2 sts, hdcblodec over the last 2 sts, sl st to first hdcblodec made, change to C. Cut B.

Rnd 9: Ch 1, hdcdec over first 2 sts (the one the ch-1 emerges from and the next), hdc in next 2 sts, (hdc, ch 2, hdc) all in next ch-2 sp, *hdc in next 2 sts, (hdcdec over next 2 sts) twice, hdc in next 2 sts, (hdc, ch 2, hdc) all in the next ch-2 sp, rep from * around until 4 sts remain, hdc in the next 2 sts, hdcdec over the last 2 sts, sl st to first hdcdec made, changing to A. Cut C.

Rnds 10-19: Rep Rnds 8-9 five more times, omitting color changes and using A for all these rnds. Do not tie off. Stop here for Toddler only and move to Rnd 1 of Hat Top to complete.

Cont to next rnds for Youth and Adult.

Rnds 20-23: Rep Rnds 8-9 two more times, omitting color changes and using A for all these rnds. Do not tie off. Stop here for Youth only and move to Rnd 1 of Hat Top to complete.

Cont to the next rnds for Adult.

Rnds 24-25: Rep Rnds 8-9 once more, omitting color change and using A for all these rnds. Do not tie off. Stop here for Adult and move to Rnd 1 of Hat Top to complete.

Hat Top

Rnd 1: Rep Rnd 8, changing to B, cut A.

Rnd 2: Rep Rnd 9, changing to C, cut B.

Rnd 3: Rep Rnd 8, changing to A, cut C.

Rnd 4: Rep Rnd 9, do not change color, cut yarn for all sizes.

FINISHING

With a tapestry needle and a length of A about 18" long, weave it in and out of each st of the last rnd created prior to Rnd 1 of Hat Top rnds. (the last rnd of A before the 2nd usage of B), pull the ends tightly to close the hat, then knot firmly. Sew around as desired to bring the top tog to your liking. Weave in all ends using the tapestry needle.

BUBBLE HUE SHIFT
Hat

Add the Chainless Foundation Row method to your skill set with this cheerful, super textured hat. Make one in either child or adult size and finish with a classic pom–pom.

FINISHED SIZES

Hat opening circumference measures approximately 18", 20".

TO FIT: Child, Adult.

YARN

Worsted weight (#4 Medium).

Shown here: Knit Picks Mighty Stitch (80% acrylic, 20% wool; 208 yards/100 grams): Silver (A), Pucker (B), Serrano (C), Orange Canary (D), Macaw (E), Gulfstream (F), Mulberry (G), 1 skein each.

HOOK

Size US G (4 mm) crochet hook.

Adjust hook size as necessary to obtain correct gauge.

NOTIONS

Basic crochet tool kit.

3" pom-pom maker or preferred tool to create pom-poms of similar size (*I used a 3" Clover Pom-Pom Maker*)

GAUGE

Checked after Row 1 and Rnd 4.

NOTES

- St counts are given as Child, (Adult). Follow the count that is in the position for the size you are making.

- Do not turn rnds unless noted.

- Mark first st of each rnd to keep track.

- During color changes, do not cut the previous colored yarn unless specified. Instead, carry the yarns you are not currently using up inside the hat loosely to minimize ends to weave in.

SPECIAL STITCHES

5 sc cluster (5sccl): (Insert hook in next dc and pull up a lp) five times total (6 lps on the hook), yo and pull through all 6 lps, ch 1. Pop cl to front if needed. When working the cl on subsequent rounds work into the ch-1 space as the stitch.

HAT

Using A, and the *"How to Work Chainless Foundation Row"* lesson on page 39, make a chainless foundation hdc row of 72 (88) sts.

GAUGE CHECK: Lay that foundation ch out and smooth it flat without stretching. At this point your piece should measure 18"(20") from end to end.

Once gauge is met, sl st to first st made to form a ring, taking care the right side of the sts is facing out and the row is not twisted. Use the beg tail to bring the bottom of the row tog.

Rnd 1: Ch 2 (does not count as a st here and throughout), bpdc around same st ch-2 emerges from, fpdc around next st, *(bpdc around next st, fpdc around next st) rep from * around, sl st to the first st while changing to B, drop A.

Rnd 2: Ch 2, bpdc around each bpdc and fpdc around each fpdc around, sl st to top of first st made.

Rnd 3: Ch 2, bpdc around each bpdc and fpdc around each fpdc around, sl st to top of first st made while changing to A, pulling it up inside the hat gently so as not to pucker the work, cut B.

Rnd 4: Ch 1 (does not count), hdc in same st and in each st around, sl st to first st made while changing to C, drop A.

GAUGE CHECK: At this point, the piece should measure 1½" tall.

Rnd 5: Ch 1, sc in same st as ch-1 and next 2 sts, 5 dc in the next st, *sc in the next 3 sts, 5 dc in the next st, rep from *around, sl st to top of first sc made while changing to D, cut C. (144 (176) sts)

Rnd 6: Ch 1, sc in same sc and in next 2 sc, 5sccl (see Special Stitches) over next 5 dc, *sc in the next

3 sc, 5sccl over the next 5 dc, rep from * around, sl st to first st while changing to A, drop D. (72 (88) sts)

Rnd 7: Ch 1 (does not count as st), hdcblo in the same sc as ch-1 and the next 2 sc, hdcblo in the next, 5sccl (remember there are 2 sts on top of each 5sccl, the close st and ch-1, you will sk the close st, and hdcblo in the ch-1), *hdcblo in the next 3 sc, hdcblo in next 5sccl, rep from * around, sl st to first st made while changing to D, drop A.

Rnd 8: Ch 1, sc in same st, 5 dc in next st, *sc in next 3 sts, 5 dc in next st, rep from * around until 2 sc rem, sc in the last 2 sc, change to E and cut D. (144 (176) sts)

Rnd 9: Ch 1, sc in same st, 5sccl over next 5 dc, *sc in next 3 sc, 5sccl over next 5 dc, rep from * around until 2 sc rem, sc in last 2 sc, sl st to first st while changing to A, drop E. (72 (88) sts)

Rnd 10: Ch 1, hdcblo same st as ch-1, hdcblo in next 5sccl taking care to sk the close st of each 5sccl and only work the ch-1, *hdcblo in next 3 sc, hdcblo in next 5sccl, rep from * around until 2 sts rem, hdcblo in each of last 2 sts, sl st to first st while changing to E, drop A.

Rnds 11-13: Rep Rnds 5-7, using E for Rnd 5, F for Rnd 6, and A for Rnd 7.

Rnds 14-16: Rep Rnds 8-10, using F for Rnd 8, G for Rnd 9, and A for Rnd 10.

Rnds 17-19: Rep Rnds 5-7, using G for Rnd 5, H for Rnd 6, and A for Rnd 7.

Rnds 20-21: Rep Rnds 8-9, using H for both, switch to A at end of Rnd 9 and cut H.

Rem of hat worked in spiral, do not join rnds.

Rnd 22: Ch 1, hdcblo in each st around, remembering to only work ch-1 on the 5sccl.

Rnd 23: (hdc in next 2 sts, hdcdec over next 2 sts) rep 18(22) times total, cont to the dec rnds for your size ONLY. (54 (66) sts)

Final Dec Rnds for Child

Rnd 24: (hdc in next 4 sts, hdc dec over next 2 sts) rep nine times total. (45 sts)

Rnd 25: (hdc in next 3 sts, hdc dec over next 2 sts) rep nine times total. (36 sts)

Rnd 26: (hdc dec over next 2 sts) rep 18 times total. (18 sts)

Rnd 27: (hdc dec over next 2 sts) rep nine times total, cut yarn, use tail to sew any rem hole closed. (9 sts)

Final Dec Rnds for Adult

Rnd 24: (hdc in next st, hdcdec over next 2 sts) rep 22 times total. (44 sts)

Rnd 25: (hdc in next 3 sts, hdcdec over next 2 sts) eight times total, hdc in next 2 hdc, hdcdec over last 2 hdc. (35 sts)

Rnd 26: (hdc in next 3 sts, hdc dec over next 2 sts) rep seven times total. (28 sts)

Rnd 27: (hdc in next 2 sts, hdc dec over next 2 sts) rep seven times total. (21 sts)

Rnd 28: (hdc in next st, hdc dec over next 2 sts) rep seven times total. (14 sts)

Rnd 29: (hdc dec over next 2 sts) rep seven times total, cut yarn, use tail to sew any rem hole closed. (7 sts)

FINISHING

Weave in all ends.

Pom-Poms

Create an optional pom-pom using the pom-pom maker (Fig. 1) or your preferred method. Using the tails from making the pom-pom, sew it to the top of the hat. Weave in any rem ends.

Fig. 1

How To Work
Chainless Foundation Row

A Chainless Foundation row is beneficial because the bottom and top of ch look identical offering a cleaner look to work and easier to edge. Whereas a ch can "bind" the first row, a chainless foundation row has the same stretch and give as the main body of the work. Here we will work a Chainless Foundation Row using HDC.

1 Ch 2, yo, insert hook in 2nd ch from hook, yo and pull up a lp (3 lps on hook).

2 Yo and ch 1 pulling through 1 lp only. This builds the bottom of the st, replacing the traditional ch.

3 Yo and pull through all 3 lps on the hook to complete the first st.

4 Yo, insert the hook under the 2 lps at the base of the st just completed as shown in Fig. 1.

5 Yo and pull up a lp, then ch 1 through 1 lp only to build the bottom of the next st. Yo again and pull through all 3 lps to complete the 2nd st. Rep steps 4-5, until the desired number of sts is achieved. Do not count the initial sk ch as a st.

Fig. 1

ASYMMETRIC OWL
Wrap

Classic chevrons take on a new twist in this owl themed costuming wrap. Wider at one end and tapering at the other, the visual interest is undeniable. Use your imagination to turn this into any character your heart desires: a unicorn, a bear—the possibilities are limitless!

FINISHED SIZE

Wrap measures approximately 68" at widest point, and 25½" from top of hood to center bottom of middle.

YARN

Worsted weight (#4 Medium).

Shown here: Knit Picks Brava Worsted (100% acrylic; 219 yards/100 grams): Cream (A), 3 skeins; Brindle (B), Persimmon (C), Caution (D), Paprika (E), Cobblestone Heather (F), Almond (G), Black (H), 1 skein each.

HOOKS

Size US H (5mm) crochet hook.

Size US E (3.5mm) crochet hook.

Adjust hook sizes as necessary to obtain correct gauge.

NOTIONS

Basic crochet tool kit.

GAUGE

14 sts x 7 rows = 4" x 4" in dc.

NOTES

• Place a marker in the ch-1 sps and in the hdc and sc reps. These ch-1s are difficult to see on subsequent rnds and st placement is critical to a chevron success. Move the marker to each new ch-1 sp from the previous rnd as you reach the previously placed markers. You may stop using them as you become familiar with the pattern, but initial use is critical to setting up placement.

• Use Size US H (5mm) crochet hook for entire pattern except eye pupil where you will use Size US E (3.5mm) crochet hook.

• During color changes, do not cut the previous colored yarn unless specified.

• The hood is created by joining Row 1 of hood to the main wrap as specified below, working in a flat rectangle, then joining with a short seam to close.

• Ears are worked in a spiral, do not turn or join rnds unless instructed.

SPECIAL STITCHES

Beginning double crochet decrease (begdcdec): Ch 2 (counts as first st), turn, yo insert hook in next st after ch-2 emerges from, yo and pull up a lp, (yo and pull through 2 lps) two times. Dec complete. On subsequent rows make sure you do not accidentally work the dec two times, it can look like 2 sts on some rows even when it is just one. If stated to begdcdecflo, then work the same but in the front lps only of the 2nd st.

MAIN WRAP

Using A, ch 183.

Row 1: Dc in 4th ch from hook, sk chs count as first dc, dc in next 11 chs, *ch 1, sk next ch, dc in next 13 chs*, rep *-* marking the 6th dc of the 13 for hood placement later, rep *-* four more times, (ch 1, sk next ch, hdc in next 13 chs) four times total, (ch 1, sk next ch, sc in next 13 chs) two times total. (169 sts and 12 ch-1 sps)

Row 2: Ch 1, turn, sc in first 6 sts, (sc, ch 1, sc) in next st, sc in next 6 sts, ch 1, sk next ch-1 sp, sc in next 6 sts, (sc, ch 1, sc) in next st, sc in next 6 sts, ch 1, sk next ch-1 sp, (hdc in next 6 sts, <hdc, ch 1, hdc> in next st, hdc in next 6 sts, ch 1, sk next ch-1 sp) four times total, (dc in next 6 sts, <dc, ch 1, dc> in next st, dc in next 6 sts, ch 1, sk next ch-1 sp) seven times total, eliminating final "ch 1, sk next ch-1 sp" on final rep. (196 sts)

Row 3: Ch 2 (counts as first dc), turn, dc in next 6 sts, (dc, ch 1, dc) in next ch-1 sp, dc in next 7 sts, ch 1, sk next ch-1 sp, (dc in next 7 sts, <dc, ch 1, dc> in next ch-1 sp, dc in next 7 sts, ch 1, sk next ch-1 sp) six times total, (hdc in next 7 sts, <hdc, ch 1, hdc> in next ch-1 sp, hdc in next 7 sts , ch 1, sk next ch-1 sp) four times total, sc in next 7 sts, <sc, ch 1, sc> in next ch-1 sp, sc in next 7 sts, ch 1, sk next ch-1 sp, sc in next 7 sts, (sc, ch 1, sc) in next ch-1 sp, sc in last 7 sts, change to B, cut A. (224 sts)

Row 4: Ch 1, turn, scblo in first 8 sts, (sc, ch 1, sc) in next ch-1 sp, scblo in next 8 sts, ch 1, sk next ch-1 sp, scblo in next 8 sts, (sc, ch 1, sc) in next ch-1 sp, scblo in next 8 sts, (ch 1, sk next ch-1 sp, hdcblo in next 8 sts, <hdc, ch 1, hdc> in next ch-1 sp, hdcblo in next 8 sts) four times total, (ch 1, sk next ch-1 sp, dcblo in next 8 sts, <dc, ch 1, dc> in next ch-1 sp, dcblo in next 8 sts) seven times total. (252 sts)

Row 5: Ch 2 (counts as first dc), turn, dc in next 8 sts, <dc, ch 1, dc> in ch-1 sp, dc in next 9 sts, ch 1, sk ch-1 sp, (dc in next 9 sts, <dc, ch 1, dc> in next ch-1 sp, dc in next 9 sts, ch 1, sk next ch-1 sp) six times total, (hdc in next 9 sts, <hdc, ch 1, hdc> in next ch-1 sp, hdc in next 9 sts, ch 1, sk next ch-1

sp) four times total, (sc in next 9 sts, <sc, ch 1, sc> in next ch-1 sp, sc in next 9 sts, ch 1, sk next ch-1 sp) two times total, eliminating final ch-1/sk on last rep, change to C, cut B.

Row 6: Ch 1, turn, scblodec over first 2 sts, scblo in next 8 sts, (sc, ch 1, sc) in next ch-1 sp, scblo in next 8 sts, scblodec over next 2 sts, ch 1, sk next ch-1 sp, scblodec over next 2 sts, scblo in next 8 sts, (sc, ch1, sc) in next ch-1 sp, scblo in next 8 sts, scdec over next 2 sts, ch 1, sk next ch-1 sp, (hdcblodec over next 2 sts, hdcblo in next 8 sts, <hdc, ch 1, hdc> in next ch-1 sp, hdcblo in next 8 sts, hdcblodec over next 2 sts, ch 1, sk next ch-1 sp) four times total, (dcblodec over next 2 sts, dcblo in next 8 sts, <dc, ch 1, dc> in next ch-1 sp, dcblo in next 8 sts, dcblodec over next 2 sts, ch 1, sk next ch-1 sp) seven times total, eliminating the final ch-1/sk on the last rep, change to A, cut C.

Row 7: Ch 2 (counts as first dc), turn, dcflo in next 9 sts, <dc, ch 1, dc> in ch-1 sp, dcflo in next 10 sts, ch 1, sk ch-1 sp, (dcflo in next 10 sts, <dc, ch 1, dc> in next ch-1 sp, dcflo in next 10 sts, ch 1, sk next ch-1 sp) six times total, (hdcflo in next 10 sts, <hdc, ch 1, hdc> in next ch-1 sp, hdcflo in next 10 sts , ch 1, sk next ch-1 sp) four times total, (scflo in next 10 sts, <sc, ch 1, sc> in next ch-1 sp, scflo in next 10 sts, ch 1, sk next ch-1 sp) two times total, eliminating final ch-1/sk on last rep.

Row 8: Ch 1, turn, scdec over first 2 sts, sc in next 9 sts, <sc, ch 1, sc> in next ch-1 sp, sc in next 9 sts, scdec over next 2 sts, ch 1, sk next ch-1 sp, scdec over next 2 sts, sc in next 9 sts, <sc, ch1, sc> in next ch-1 sp, sc in next 9 sts, scdec over next 2 sts, ch 1, sk next ch-1 sp, (hdcdec over next 2 sts, hdc in next 9 sts, <hdc, ch 1, hdc> in next ch-1 sp, hdc in next 9 sts, hdcdec over next 2 sts, ch 1, sk next ch-1 sp) four times total, (dcdec over next 2 sts, dc in next 9 sts, <dc, ch 1, dc> in next ch-1 sp, dc in next 9 sts, dcdec over next 2 sts, ch 1, sk next ch-1 sp) seven

times total, eliminating the final ch-1/sk on the last rep, change to D, cut A.

Row 9: Begdcdecflo (see Special Stitches) over first 2 sts, dcflo in next 9 sts, <dc, ch 1, dc> in next ch-1 sp, dcflo in next 9 sts, dcflodec over next 2 sts, ch 1, sk next ch-1 sp, (dcflodec over next 2 sts, dc in next 9 sts, <dc, ch 1, dc> in next ch-1 sp, dcflo in next 9 sts, dcflodec over next 2 sts, ch 1, sk next ch-1 sp) six times total, (hdcflodec over next 2 sts, hdcflo in next 9 sts, <hdc, ch 1, hdc> in next ch-1 sp, hdcflo in next 9 sts, hdcflodec over next 2 sts, ch 1, sk next ch-1 sp) four times total, scflodec over next 2 sts, scflo in next 9 sts, <sc, ch 1, sc> in next ch-1 sp, scflo in next 9 sts, scflodec over next 2 sts, ch 1, sk next ch-1 sp, scflodec over next 2 sts, scflo in next 9 sts, <sc, ch 1, sc> in next ch-1 sp, scflo in next 9 sts, scflodec over last 2 sts, change to E, cut D.

Row 10: Ch 1, turn, scblodec over first 2 sts, scblo in next 9 sts, <sc, ch 1, sc> in next ch-1 sp, scblo in next 9 sts, scblodec over next 2 sts, ch 1, sk next ch-1 sp, scblodec over next 2 sts, scblo in next 9 sts, <sc, ch1, sc> in next ch-1 sp, scblo in next 9 sts, scblodec over next 2 sts, ch 1, sk next ch-1 sp, (hdcblodec over next 2 sts, hdcblo in next 9 sts, <hdc, ch 1, hdc> in next ch-1 sp, hdcblo in next 9 sts, hdcblodec over next 2 sts, ch 1, sk next ch-1 sp) four times total, (dcblodec over next 2 sts, dcblo in next 9 sts, <dc, ch 1, dc> in next ch-1 sp, dcblo in next 9 sts, dcblodec over next 2 sts, ch 1, sk next ch-1 sp) seven times total, eliminating the final ch-1/sk on the last rep.

Row 11: Begdcdec over first 2 sts, dc in next 9 sts, <dc, ch 1, dc> in next ch-1 sp, dc in next 9 sts, dcdec over next 2 sts, ch 1, sk next ch-1 sp, (dcdec over next 2 sts, dc in next 9 sts, <dc, ch 1, dc> in next ch-1 sp, dc in next 9 sts, dcdec over next 2 sts, ch 1, sk next ch-1 sp) six times total, (hdcdec over next 2 sts, hdc in next 9 sts, <hdc, ch 1, hdc> in next ch-1 sp, hdc in next 9 sts, hdcdec over next 2 sts, ch 1, sk next ch-1 sp) four times total, scdec over next 2 sts, sc in next 9 sts, <sc, ch 1, sc> in next ch-1 sp, sc in next 9 sts, scdec over next 2 sts, ch 1, sk next ch-1 sp, scdec over next 2 sts, sc in next 9 sts, <sc, ch 1, sc> in next ch-1 sp, sc in next 9 sts, scdec over last 2 sts, change to F, cut E.

Row 12: Using F, rep Row 10.

Row 13: Rep Row 11.

Row 14: Rep Row 8, change to D, cut F.

Row 15: Rep Row 9, change to B, cut D.

Row 16: Rep Row 10.

Row 17: Rep Row 11, change to G, cut B.

Row 18: Rep Row 10, change to C, cut G.

Row 19: Rep Row 9, change to E, cut C.

Note: *If you are feeling adventurous, a longer cape can be made by adding rows at this point before Row 20.*

Row 20: Ch 1, turn, scflodec over first 2 sts, scflo in next 9 sts, <sc, ch 1, sc> in next ch-1 sp, scflo in next 9 sts, scflodec over next 2 sts, ch 1, sk next ch-1 sp, scflodec over next 2 sts, scflo in next 9 sts, <sc, ch1, sc> in next ch-1 sp, scflo in next 9 sts, scflodec over next 2 sts, ch 1, sk next ch-1 sp, (hdcflodec over next 2 sts, hdcflo in next 9 sts, <hdc, ch 1, hdc> in next ch-1 sp, hdcflo in next 9 sts, hdcflodec over next 2 sts, ch 1, sk next ch-1 sp) four times total, (dcflodec over next 2 sts, dcflo in next 9 sts, <dc, ch 1, dc> in next ch-1 sp, dcflo in next 9 sts, dcflodec over next 2 sts, ch 1, sk next ch-1 sp) seven times total, eliminating the final ch-1/sk on the last rep, cut yarn.

HOOD

Note: *The hood is not centered so the narrow end can drape and dangle down. Feel free to adjust hood to center position if you prefer.*

First Half

With the ridged side (the side that has texture created by the front and back lp sts) of main wrap facing up and Row 1 furthest from your hands, join A in the *bottom* of the marked st from Row 1 of Main Wrap. You are working along the base of the ch of Row 1 in the rem lps from the beg ch.

Row 1: Ch 2 (counts as dc here and throughout), dc in next 73 sts (work both the sts and the ch-1 sps). (74 dc)

Rows 2-25: Ch 2 (mark the ch-2 on Row 25 only for placement later), turn, dc in each st across. (74 sts)

Row 26 (Partial Row, begin hood shaping first half): Ch 2, turn, dc in next 34 sts, dcdec over next 2 sts. (36 sts)

Row 27: Begdcdc over first 2 sts, dcdec over next 2 sts, dc in next 32 sts. (34 sts)

Row 28: Ch 2, turn, dc in next 31 sts, dcdec over last 2 sts. (33 sts)

Row 29: Begdcdec over first 2 sts, dc in last 31 sts. (32 sts)

Row 30: Ch 2, turn, dc in next 29 sts, hdcdec over last 2 sts, do not cut yarn, cont to work down ends of rows to edge them, ch 1, work 1 sc in the side of the hdc just made, work 2 sc around the post on the side of each of the next 4 rows, sl st to st at base of last dc, cut yarn leaving 36" tail for sewing. (31 sts in the row plus 9 sc down the side)

Second Half

Position piece so ridged side of main wrap is facing up and the main wrap closer to your hands and the hood is further. Join A with a sl st in the end marked st from Row 25.

Rep Row 26 from Hood First Half without turning at the beg of the row.

Rep Rows 27-30 from Hood First Half.

Close Hood

Using the end tail from either side of the hood, fold it in half matching Row 30 from both sides to each other. Make sure you fold with the ridged side of the main wrap facing out. Using a tapestry needle and mattress st, sew the free edges tog. First, sew the sc that were worked in the ends of the rows, then across Row 30. Weave in all ends to this point.

Edging

Position piece so the right (ridged) side of the main wrap and right (outside) of hood are facing up with the hood furthest from you and the DC end of the main wrap to the right.

Row 1: Join A with a sl st in the st of the main wrap just prior to the first st of the Hood Row 1, ch 1, work 2 sc around the post of each dc at the end of each of the 30 rows up the hood to the center seam, sc in the st of the center seam, work 2 sc around the post of each dc at the end of each of the 30 rows down the second side of the hood, sl st into the next 2 sts on the main wrap. (121 sts, not counting sl sts)

Row 2: Ch 1, turn, sk the 2 sl sts, scflo in each st across the hood, at end ch-1, sk the first sl st made in Row 1 and sl st in the next st on the main wrap.

Row 3: Ch 1, turn, sk the sl sts, scblo in each st across the hood, at end sl st into the ch-1 from beg of Row 2, sl st in next st on main wrap, cut yarn.

OWL EYES

Note: *Do not turn or join rnds unless instructed.*

Layer 1 (Make 2)
Using F, make magic ring (see Magic Ring on page 17), ch 1.

Rnd 1: Sc 6 in ring, pull tail tightly to close ring. (6 sc)

Rnd 2: Sc 2 in each sc around. (12 sc)

Rnd 3: (sc in next sc, 2 sc in next sc) six times total. (18 sc)

Rnd 4: (sc in next 2 sc, 2 sc in next sc) six times total. (24 sc)

Rnd 5: (sc in next 3 sc, 2 sc in next sc) six times total, sl st first st made. (30 sc)

Rnd 6: Ch 1, sc in same sc as ch-1, sc in next sc, hdc in next st, 3 dc in next st, hdc in next st, (sc in next 2 sts, hdc in next st, 3 dc in next st, hdc in next st) five times total, sl st to first sc made, cut yarn leaving long tail for sewing. (6 "petals")

Layer 2 (Make 2)
Using C, make magic ring, ch 1.

Rnds 1-4: Rep Rnds 1-4 of Layer 1.

Rnd 5: Sl st to next st, ch 1, sc in same st as ch-1, (hdc, dc) in next st, (dc, hdc) in next st, sc in next st, (sc in next st, <hdc, dc> in next st, <dc, hdc> in next st, sc in next st) five times total, sl st to first st made, cut yarn leaving long tail for sewing. (6 "petals")

Layer 3 (Make 2)
Using G, make magic ring, ch 1.

Rnds 1-4: Rep Rnds 1-4 of Layer 1, after Rnd 4, sl st to first st made, cut yarn leaving long tail for sewing.

Layer 4 (Make 2)

Using D, make magic ring, ch 1.

Rnds 1-2: Rep Rnds 1-2 of Layer 1, after Rnd 2, sl st to first st made, cut yarn.

Rnd 3: Turn the circle over so the wrong side of the sts are facing up. Join H with a sl st in any flo around, ch 1, sl st loosely in each flo around, sl st to first sl st made.

Rnd 4: Turn the circle so the right side of the sts of Rnds 1-2 are facing up, ch 1, sl st in each sl st around, sl st to first sl st made, cut yarn leaving long tail for sewing.

Pupil (Make 2)

Using H and Size US E (3.5 mm) crochet hook, make magic ring, ch 1.

Rnd 1: Sc 6 in ring, sl st to first st made, pull tail tightly to close ring, cut yarn leaving long tail for sewing. (6 sc)

EARS (MAKE 2)

With A held double stranded, make magic ring, ch 1.

Rnd 1: Sc 4 in ring, pull tail tightly to close. (4 sc)

Rnd 2: Sc in each sc around.

Rnd 3: (sc in next sc, 2 sc in next sc) twice. (6 sc)

Rnd 4: (sc in next 2 sc, 2 sc in next sc) twice. (8 sc)

Rnd 5: (sc in next sc, 2 sc in next sc) four times total. (12 sc)

Rnd 6: (sc in next 5 sc, 2 sc in next sc) twice. (14 sc)

Rnd 7: (sc in next 6 sc, 2 sc in next sc) twice. (16 sc)

Rnds 8-9: Sc in each st around, at end of Rnd 9, sl st to first sc made, cut yarn leaving long tail for sewing.

Tufts

Cut 6" strands of A, G, C, and F. Insert your hook around any of the sts at the small tip of the ear. Align all the strands tog evenly and fold them in half. Lay the lp end on your hook and pull through the tip of the ear. Pull the loose ends through the lp and tug tightly to secure. Trim evenly. Rep for the other ear.

BEAK

Using D held double stranded, ch 4.

Row 1: Sc in 2nd ch from hook and each ch to end. (3 sc)

Rows 2-3: Ch 1, turn, sc in each st across.

Row 4: Ch 1, turn, sc in first st, scdec over last 2 sts. (2 sts)

Row 5: Ch 1, turn, scdec over the 2 sts, do not cut yarn, cont to Edge Rnd. (1 sts)

Edge Rnd: Ch 1, turn, sc in the end of the 4 rows, 3 sc in first st at base of Row 1, sc in next st, 3 sc in last st, sc in the end of the 4 rows up the 2nd side, (sc, ch 2, sl st in 2nd ch from hook, sc) all in the sc of Row 4, sl st to first st made, cut yarn leaving tail for sewing.

FINISHING

Stack the layers of the eye tog with Layer 1 on the bottom, Layer 2 on top of that, Layer 3 on top of that, Layer 4 on top of Layer 3, and ending with the pupil on the top. Sew the eyes tog.

Note: Sew tog making sure that the petals of Layer 2 are alternating with the petals on Layer 1 and not matched up. Weave in all ends except the long tail from Layer 1.

Using picture on page 46 as a reference, sew the eyes on the hood. Notice how on Layer 3, at the color change, it has a spot where the rnds meet up jagged and create an "eye sparkle" detail. Using pins to help with placement, position the eyes on the hood with the bottom of the eye about 4 sts behind the hood edging and 2 rows on either side of the center seam. Make sure the "eye sparkles" face the 2 o'clock position on the right eye and the 11 o'clock position on the left eye. Sew in place using the tail from Layer 1.

Use pins to help with placement determination of ears. When satisfied, sew one ear to either side of the hood with them *slightly* open at the base. They are 3 sts behind the topmost part of Layer 1 of the eye and 3 rows to either side of the center hood seam. 6 rows are bet the innermost edge of the ears. Sew in any rem ends.

Using the long end tail, sew the beak bet the eyes so half is bet the eyes and half is below the eyes. Gently cup the beak up as you sew it on to add dimension. Weave in any rem ends.

PLAYTIME
Projects

There's nothing quite as special as a handmade toy. These heirloom-worthy patterns are fun and exciting to crochet and sure to make any youngster or young at heart adult in your life happy as can be!

52

56

66

72

78

86

HAPPY HEART
Bunting

Sure to bright up any party, playroom, or even a workspace, this adorable heart bunting will make you happy any time you look at it!

Simple granny–square–style hearts and tiny dangling poms–poms make this project both colorful and quick! Easily customize your bunting by playing with color combinations or changing the quantity of hearts to make it longer or shorter.

FINISHED SIZE

Bunting measures approximately 96" long.

YARN

Bulky weight (#5 Bulky).

Shown here: Knit Picks Brava Bulky (100% acrylic; 136 yards/100 grams): White (A), Rouge, Red, Orange, Canary, Peapod, Celestial, and Eggplant, 1 skein each.

HOOK

Size US H (5 mm) crochet hook.

Adjust hook size as necessary to obtain correct gauge.

NOTIONS

Basic crochet tool kit.

¾" and 1⅜" pom-pom maker or preferred tool to create pom-poms of similar size (*I used an Extra Small Clover Pom-Pom Maker in ¾" and Small Clover Pom-Pom Maker in 1⅜"*).

GAUGE

While not critical, each heart should be about 4.5" at their widest point across so they hang nicely, and you maintain yarn quantities stated.

NOTES

- To make a bunting like the one shown, make two hearts of each of the eight colors for a total of 16 hearts.

- Do not turn rnds, mark the first st of the rnd to keep track as needed.

HEARTS

Begin by making magic ring. (See Magic Ring on Page 17).

Rnd 1: Ch 1 (does not count as a st here and throughout), 3 hdc in ring, ch 2, *3 hdc in the ring, ch 2, rep from *, two more times, sl st to first hdc made. (12 hdc)

Rnd 2: Slstblo across the next 2 hdc, sl st into the next ch-2 sp, ch 1, (3 hdc, ch 2, 3 hdc) in the same sp ch 1, *(3 hdc, ch 2, 3 hdc) in the next ch-2 sp, ch 1, rep from * two more times, sl st to first hdc made. (24 hdc)

Rnd 3: Slstblo across the next 2 hdc, sl st in to the next ch-2 sp, ch 1, 6 hdc in the same sp, ch 1, sk next 3 hdc, 3 hdc in the next ch-1 sp, ch 2, sk next 3 hdc, (sc, ch 1, sc) in the next ch-2 sp, ch 2, sk next 3 hdc, 3 hdc in the next ch-1 sp, ch 1, sk next 3 hdc, 6 hdc in the next ch-2 sp, ch 1, sk next 3 hdc, 3 hdc in the next ch-1 sp, ch 1, sk next 3 hdc, (3 hdc, ch 2, 3 hdc) in the next ch-2 sp, ch 1, sk next 3 hdc, 3 hdc in the next ch-1 sp, ch 1, sl st to first hdc made. (32 sts)

Rnd 4: Slstblo across the next 2 hdc, sc in the next st, hdc in the next st, 2 dc in the next st, sk the next ch-1 sp and hdc, (3 tr/7 dc) all in the next st, sk the next hdc, sk next ch-2 sp, sk next sc, and sl st in the ch-1 sp bet the 2 sc, sk the next sc, sk next ch-2 sp, sk next hdc, (7 dc/3 tr) all in the next st, sk the next hdc and ch-1 sp, 2 dc in the next st, hdc in the next st, sc in the next st, sl st in the next 2 sts, sl st into next sp, cut yarn leaving a long tail for sewing later.

POM-POMS

Make one smaller and one larger pom-pom in each of the eight colors listed, for a total of 16 pom-poms. Do not trim the ends that result from securing the centers, these will be used later in the pattern.

FINISHING

Using A, ch a strand of basic chs that is 8 feet in length. Weave the ends back into the ch and trim flush.

Using color and pom-pom placement of your choice, attached hearts and pom-poms as folls:

Attach the Hearts

Space the hearts along the ch strand evenly spaced in the order of your choice, pinning in place to secure. The pattern shows basic rainbow order in a double rep from left to right. Making sure the right side of the heart is facing up and using the tail end from the heart, sew the center tr of the 3tr in the 7dc/3tr grouping on the left side of the heart to the ch strand to secure. Weave the tails into the heart and trim flush. Rep with each heart across the strand. (If you plan to hang doubled right to left, then left to right as shown in the main pattern image: you will want the second half of your hearts to be sewn on with the wrong side of the sts facing front. That way when you hang the second half, the right side of the sts faces front.)

Attach the Pom-Poms

Using the tail ends from the larger pom-poms and tapestry needle, sew the larger pom-poms below and hanging about 2" from the smaller pom-poms of the same color. Sew through the wrapped center of the pom-poms by feel as you are able to secure well. Once sewn in place, trim the ends flush with the smaller pom-poms so they blend in. Rep this for all the pom-poms, pairing the small and large of same color tog. Attach the pom-poms to the pointed base tip of each heart of the same color in an alternating pattern. Rep this across, referring to photo for color placement guidance as needed. Weave in all rem ends.

FOLDABLE
Hamburger

A toy? A scarf? How about both! Each part of the burger is created separately allowing you to make as many toppings as you wish. Join them using the simple mattress stitch taught in this pattern and get to wearing the most fun scarf you will ever own!

FINISHED SIZE

Unfolded, burger measures approximately 40" long.

YARN

Worsted weight (#4 Medium).

Shown here: Red Heart Super Saver and With Love (100% acrylic; 370 yards/198 grams): Gold (A), Buff (B), Spring Green (C), Cherry Red (D), White (E), Dark Orchid (F), Evergreen (G), Yellow (H), Red (I), Berry Red (J), Pumpkin (K), Coffee (L), Warm Brown (M), 1 skein each.

HOOK

Size US G (4.25 mm) crochet hook.

Adjust hook size as necessary to obtain correct gauge.

NOTIONS

Basic crochet tool kit.

Small amount of polyester stuffing.

GAUGE

Measure after first bottom bun half is completed using instructions within pattern.

NOTES

· Do not turn or join rnds unless instructed.

· Mark rnds with a stitch marker to keep track.

· Ch do not count as st unless specifically stated.

· During color changes, do not cut the previous colored yarn unless specified.

BUN (MAKE 2)
Bun Base
Using A, make magic ring. (See Magic Ring on page 17).

Rnd 1: Ch 1, 8 sc in ring, pull tail to close. (8 sc)

Rnd 2: Sc 2 in each st around. (16 sc)

Rnd 3: (sc in next st, 2 sc in next st) eight times total. (24 sc)

Rnd 4: (sc in next st, 2 sc in next st, sc in next st) eight times total. (32 sc)

Rnd 5: (2 sc in next st, sc in next 3 sts) eight times total. (40 sc)

Rnd 6: (2 sc in next st, sc in next 4 sts) eight times total, sl st to first st made, do not cut cont to flap. (48 sc)

Create Join Flap
Row 1: Ch 1, turn, sc in same st the ch-1 emerges from and next 3 sts. (4 sc)

Row 2: Ch 1, turn, sc in each st across, cut yarn leaving tail for sewing later.

Edge Round
Rnd 1: With wrong side of the bun's sts facing up, join yarn with sl st in the blo of the st just right of the flap, ch 1, revscblo (see Reverse Single Crochet on page 15) in same st as ch-1 and in each st around until you reach the opposite side of the flap, cut yarn.

Weave in all ends except the one on the flap. Sew the edge rounds tails strategically to make a smooth join bet the edge and the flap.

GAUGE CHECK: While gauge is not super critical, you do want to be sure you have nice tight sts so the project looks the same when completed. The bun base when completed measures just under 3¾" across not including the flap.

Bun Top
Note: *I prefer the symmetry of two buns with seeds, so technically two top buns. But if you prefer a top bun and "bottom bun," create one as written for the top bun and one as written but eliminate Rnd 8 and the sesame seeds for the bottom bun.*

Rnds 1-6: Rep Rnds 1-6 of Bun Base. (40 sts after round 5)

Rnds 7-8: Sc in each st around, after round 8 sl st to first st made and cut yarn leaving a long tail for sewing. (48 sts)

Using B and tapestry needle, sew small straight stitches 1 sc in length to simulate the seeds. Do not worry how the underside looks, it will be hidden once sewn tog.

Place the bun top on top of the bun base, the right side of the bun top should face out and be on top of the wrong side of the sts of the bun base just inside the revsc rnd. Using the tail, sew ¾ of the way around through the rem lp on the bun base and the both lps on the bun top matching stitch for stitch, attaching the two. Stuff gently to hold shape and complete sewing all the way around. Weave in tails.

LETTUCE
Using C, make magic ring.

Rnd 1: Ch 1, 8 sc in ring, pull tail to close ring. (8 sc)

Rnd 2: Sc 2 in each sc around. (16 sc)

Rnd 3: (sc in next st, 2 sc in next st) eight times total. (24 sc)

Rnd 4: (sc in next 2 sts, 2 sc in next st) eight times total, sl st to first st made. (32 sc)

Rnd 5: Ch 3 (counts as first dc), dc 2 in same st as ch-3, dc 3 in each st around, sl st to top of beg ch-3. (96 dc)

Rnd 6: Ch 1, hdc in same st as ch-1, hdc in each st around, sl st to first hdc made, do not cut, cont to Flap 1.

Flap 1
Row 1: Ch 1, sc in same st as ch-1, sc in next 3 sts. (4 sc)

Row 2: Ch 1, turn, sc in each st across, cut yarn leaving tail for sewing.

Flap 2
Row 1: With right side of sts facing up and Flap 1 to the right, count 45 sts left from the top edge of Flap 1, rejoin yarn in the 45th st left with a sl st, ch 1, sc in same st as ch-1 and next 3 sts. (4 sts)

Row 2: Ch 1, turn, sc in each st across, cut yarn leaving a tail for sewing later.

TOMATO
Using D, make magic ring.

Rnd 1: Ch 1, 8 sc in ring, pull tail to close ring. (8 sc)

Rnd 2: Sc 2 in each st around. (16 sc)

Rnd 3: (sc in next st, 2 sc in next st) eight times total, sl st to first st made. (24 sc)

Rnd 4: Ch 4 (counts as hdc/ch-2), sk next st, hdc in next st, (hdc next st, ch 2, sk next st, hdc next st) seven times total, sl st to 2nd ch of beg ch-4. (16 hdc and 8 ch-2 sps)

Rnd 5: Ch 1, sc in same st as ch-1, 3 sc in the ch-2 sp, (sc in next 2 hdc, 3 sc in next ch-2 sp) seven times total, sc in last hdc, sl st to first st made, do not cut, cont to Flap 1. (40 sts)

Flap 1

Row 1: Ch 1, sc in same st as ch-1 and next 3 sts. (4 sc)

Row 2: Ch 1, turn, sc in each sc, cut yarn leaving tail for sewing.

Flap 2

Row 1: Position piece so right side of sts are facing up and Flap 1 is to the right. Count 17 sts left from the top edge of Flap 1 and join yarn with a sl st in the 17th st, ch 1, sc in same st as ch-1 and next 3 sts. (4 sts)

Row 2: Ch 1, turn, sc in each st across, cut yarn leaving long tail for sewing.

PURPLE ONION

Using E, make magic ring with a longer end tail than normal.

Rnd 1: Ch 1, 16 sc in ring, do not pull ring closed. Weave the longer than normal end tail very securely in this rnd's sts to keep it secure but open in center. (16 sc)

Rnd 2: (sc in next st, 2 sc in next st) eight times total, sl st to blo only of first st made. (24 sc)

Rnd 3: (scblo in next 2 sts, 2scblo in next st) eight times total. (32 scblo)

Rnd 4: (sc in next 3 sts, 2 sc in next st) eight times total, sl st to blo only of the first st changing to F at final yo of last st, cut E. (40 sc)

Rnd 5: (scblo in next 4 sts, 2 scblo in next st) eight times total, sl st to first st made, do not cut yarn, cont to Flap 1. (48 scblo)

Flap 1

Row 1: Ch 1, sc in same st as ch-1 and next 3 sts. (4 sc)

Row 2: Ch 1, turn, sc in each st across, cut yarn leaving tail for sewing.

Flap 2

Row 1: Position piece so right side of sts are facing up and Flap 1 is to the right, count 21 sts left from the top edge of Flap 1, join yarn with a sl st in the 21st st left, ch 1, sc in same st as ch-1 and next 3 sts. (4 sts)

Row 2: Ch 1, turn, sc in each st across, cut yarn leaving long tail to sew.

Purple Ring Accent

With right side of piece facing up, join F with a sl st in any rem front lp from Rnd 3, sl st loosely in each front lp around, sl st to first sl st made and cut yarn.

PICKLES

Slice with Flap (Make 2)

Using G, make magic ring.

Rnd 1: Ch 1, 8 sc in ring, pull tail to close ring. (8 sc)

Rnd 2: Sc 2 in each st around. (16 sc)

Rnd 3: (sc in next st, 2 sc in next st) eight times total, sl st to first st made, do not cut, cont to Flap. (24 sc)

Flap

Row 1: Ch 1, sc in same st as ch-1 and next 3 sts. (4 sc)

Row 2: Ch 1, turn, sc in each st across, cut tail, leaving end for sewing.

Slice w/o Flap

Rep as for Rnds 1-3 of Slice with Flap, after Rnd 3 cut yarn leaving long tail for sewing.

Sew the 2 slices with flaps so that one flap is left center and one is right center. Lay the slice without flap in the center and on top of the other two slices. Sew all into place and then weave in all ends except the ends on the flaps.

CONDIMENTS

Mustard

Using H, and leaving a long tail, make magic ring.

Rnd 1: Ch 1, 8 sc in ring, pull tail tightly to close. (8 sc)

Rnd 2: Sc 2 in each sc around. (16 sc)

Rnd 3: (sc in next st, 2 sc in next st) eight times total. (24 sc)

Rnd 4: (sc in next, hdc in next, dc/hdc in next st) eight times total. (32 sts)

Rnd 5 (partial rnd): (sl st in next, hdc in next, dc in next, dc/hdc in next st) seven times total, leave rem sts unworked in rnd, sl st to next st, do not cut yarn, cont to Flap. (35 st)

Flap

Row 1: Ch 1, sc in same st as ch-1 and next 3 sts. (4 sc)

Row 2: Ch 1, turn, sc in each st across, cut yarn leaving tail for sewing.

Ketchup

Using I, repeat Rnds 1-5 and Flap of Mustard.

Lay one condiment on top of the other so that the flaps are positioned left and right directly across from each other. Use the tails to sew them tog overlapped. Weave in all tails except the long end flap tail.

BACON

Slices (Make 2)

Using J, ch 20.

Row 1: Hdc in 2nd bb from hook, hdc in next 3 bb, 3hdc in next bb, hdc in next 3 bb, 3hdcdec over next 3 bb (3 bb dec to 1 st), hdc in next 3 bb, 3hdc in next bb, hdc in last 4 bb change to K on final yo of last hdc, cut J. (21 sts)

Row 2: Ch 1, turn, hdcflo in first 3 sts, 2hdcdecflo over next 2 sts, 3hdcflo in next st, 2hdcdecflo over next 2 sts, 3hdcdecflo over next 3 sts, hdcflo in next 2 sts, 2hdcdecflo over next 2 sts, 3hdcflo in next st, 2hdcdecflo over next 2 sts, hdcflo in last 3 sts, change to J on final yo of last st, cut K. (19 sts)

Row 3: Ch 1, turn, hdcblo in first 3 sts, 2hdcdecblo over next 2 sts, 3hdcblo in next st, hdcblo in next st, 2hdcdecblo over next 2 sts, 3hdcdecblo over next 3 sts, hdcblo in next st, 3hdcblo in next st, 2hdcdecblo over next 2 sts, hdcblo in last 3 sts, cut yarn. (18 sts)

Flap (Do for both slices)

With the ridged side of the slice facing up, join yarn with sl st in the st, just before the dec in the low point of the bacon.

Row 1: Ch 1, sc in same st as ch-1 and next 3 sts. (4 sc)

Row 2: Ch 1, turn, sc in each st, cut yarn leaving tail for sewing.

Using the tails, position the slices so the ridged side is facing up and the flaps are to the left and right, sew the three "peaks" tog leaving the center sts open and unsewn. The center tall peaks will slightly overlap. Weave in all tails but the long flap tail.

CHEESE SLICE

Using K, ch 11.

Row 1: Sc in 2nd bb from hook and each rem bb across. (10 sc)

Rows 2-10: Ch 1, turn, sc in each st across, do not cut, cont to Edge Rnd.

Edge Rnd: Ch 1, do not turn, sc in end of each of the 10 rows down the side, make 3 sc in first st across bottom, sc in next 8 sts, 3 sc in last st, sc in end of each of the next 10 rows, 3 sc in first st across top, sc in next 8 sts, 3 sc in last st, sl st to first st made, sl st in next 3 sts, do not cut yarn cont to Flap 1.

Flap 1

Row 1: Ch 1, sc in same st as ch-1 and next 3 sts. (4 sc)

Row 2: Ch 1, turn, sc in each st across, cut yarn leaving tail for sewing.

Flap 2

Row 1: With right side of Edge Rnd facing up and Flap 1 to the right, join the yarn with a sl st to the st in the end of the 3rd row from the top on the left edge, ch 1, sc in same st and next 3 sts.

Row 2: Ch 1, turn, sc in each st across, cut yarn leaving tail for sewing.

MEAT PATTY

Using L and M held double stranded, make magic ring.

Rnd 1: Ch 1, 8 sc in ring, pull tail to close ring. (8 sc)

Rnd 2: Sc 2 in each st around. (16 sc)

Rnd 3: (sc in next st, 2 sc in next st) eight times total. (24 sc)

Rnd 4: (sc in next st, 2 sc in next st, sc in next st) eight times total. (32 sc)

Rnd 5: (2 sc in next st, sc in next 3 sts) eight times total, sl st to first st made, do not cut yarn, cont to Flap 1. (40 sc)

Flap 1

Row 1: Ch 1, sc in same st as ch-1 and next 3 sts. (4 sc)

Row 2: Ch 1, turn, sc in each st across.

Flap 2

Row 1: Position the piece so the right side of the sts is facing up and Flap 1 is centered and to the right, count 17 sts to the left from the top edge of Flap 1, join double yarn w sl st in the 17th st left, ch 1, sc in same st as ch-1 and next 3 sts. (4 sts)

Row 2: Ch 1, turn, sc in each st across, cut yarn leaving tail for sewing.

FINISHING

Position all the pieces in the order you desire with the right side of the piece facing up, making sure you are starting with a bun and ending with a bun. I placed them in the exact order they were created in the pattern from left to right. You can make multiples of toppings if you want a longer final piece. If you add or remove toppings, you *may* have to place the last bun with the underside facing up so when it folds up accordion style, it is positioned correctly on your piece. Test by mock folding before you add the final bun half.

Using the end tails from the flaps, sew them tog and weave in any rem ends. You will want to butt the ends up to each other and use a mattress stitch inside the "V" (see *"How to Mattress Stitch"* lesson) so the join is as seamless as possible.

Use an accordion-style fold to stack the burger!

How to Mattress Stitch

Using one of the end tails from the two flaps you want to seam tog, insert the needle from the one side to the other in bet the "V" of the st from the lowest st to the st above it (Fig. 1). Sew the tail in the same manner through the "V" of the st on the opposing side. Rep alternating from side to side working within the "V" of the sts (Fig. 2).

Finally, tug the tail to bring both sides tog (Fig. 3). Notice how the differing colors come tog neatly and nearly seamlessly. Use the tail to bring the topmost sts tog, weave in tail, cut yarn.

Fig. 2

Fig. 1

Fig. 3

FOLDABLE
Hot Dog

No picnic is complete without hot dogs! Work up a "classic" dog by making the pattern as–is or make it up just how you like it by adding or removing condiments. Pair this adorable hot dog with the foldable hamburger for the perfect playtime combo!

FINISHED SIZE

Unfolded hot dog measures approximately 36" long.

YARN

Worsted weight (#4 Medium).

Shown here: Red Heart Super Saver and With Love (100% acrylic; 370 yards/198 grams): Buff (A), Gold (B), Spice Orange (C), Red (D), Yellow (E), Shaded Greens (F), White (G), 1 skein each.

HOOKS

Size US G (4.25 mm) crochet hook.

Size US H (5 mm) crochet hook.

Adjust hook sizes as necessary to obtain correct gauge.

NOTIONS

Basic crochet tool kit.

Small amount of polyester stuffing.

NOTES

- Do not turn or join rnds unless specifically instructed.

- Mark first st of each rnd, moving marker to new rnd as you proceed, to keep track.

- During color changes, do not cut the previous colored yarn unless specified.

- Work single strand unless specifically instructed to work double. Single strand parts use Size US G (4.25 mm) crochet hook, double strand parts use Size US H (5 mm) crochet hook.

- The condiment strips are worked double stranded. If you cannot find a variegated green for the relish, select 2 shades of green instead.

- Each piece aside from the bun will begin and end with a ch 3 that will be knotted and sewn tog to allow for the "folding" assembly after.

BUN

Inner Flat Bun Part (Make 2)

Using A and Size US G (4.25 mm) crochet hook, ch 20.

Rnd 1: Sc in 2nd bb from hook and next 17 bb, 3 sc in last bb, working up the opposite side of the starting ch (creating an oval shape), sc in next 17 sts, 2sc in last st. (40sc)

Rnd 2: Sc 2 in next st, sc in next 17 sts, sc 2 in each of next 3 sts, sc in next 17 sts, sc 2 in each of last 2 sc. (46 sc)

Rnd 3: Sc 2 in each of next 2 sts, sc in next 17 sts, sc 2 in each of next 2 sts, sc in next 2 sts, 2sc in each of next 2 sts, sc in next 18 sts, sc 2 in each of next 2 sts, sc in last st. (54 sc)

Rnd 4: Sc in next 2 sts, sc 2 in each of next 2 sts, sc in next 19 sts, sc 2 in next st, sc in next st, sc 2 in next st, sc in next 2 sts, sc 2 in next st, sc in next st, sc 2 in next st, sc in next 20 sts, sc 2 in next st, sc in last 2 sts. (61 sc)

Rnd 5: Sc in next 3 sts, sc 2 in next st, sc in next 23 sts, 2sc in next st, sc in next 5 sts, sc 2 in next st, sc in next 23 sts, sc 2 in next st, sc in last 3 sts, sl st to first st made, cut yarn. (65 sc)

Rounded Top Bun Part (Make 2)

Using B and Size US G (4.25 mm) crochet hook, ch 20.

Rnds 1-5: Rep same as Rnds 1-5 of Inner Flat Bun, but do not cut yarn after Rnd 5. (65 sts)

Rnd 6: Ch 1, do not turn, sc in same st as ch-1 and each st around, sl st to first st made.

Rnd 7: Ch 1, do not turn, sc in same st as ch-1 and each st around, sl st to first st made, cut yarn leaving long tail for sewing.

Joining Rnd

With Size US G (4.25 mm) crochet hook, place one top bun on one flat bottom bun with the wrong sides touching and facing in aligning st for st (there are 65 sts on the last rnd of each bun half).

Insert hook through both lps of the top bun in any st around, then through the matching st in the front/inner lp only of the bottom bun.

Join B with a sl st, ch 1, sc through all the lps at once to join them, sc in each matching pair of sts around in the same manner (both lps top bun/inner lp bottom bun), once about ¾ of the way around, stuff the bun with polyester stuffing, complete the rnd and sl st to first st made, cut yarn.

Rep for second half.

Weave in ends. Place both halves tog with light tan inner buns touching. Using a separate strand of B and working through Join Rnd of both halves, sew the sts of one long side tog so the bun hinges open and shut like a real hot dog bun. Weave in ends.

HOT DOG

Using C and Size US G (4.25 mm) crochet hook, ch 5, then make magic ring (see Magic Ring on page 17), leaving an 8" tail.

Rnd 1: Ch 1, 6 sc in ring. (6 sc)

Rnd 2: Sc 2 in each sc around. (12 sc)

Note: Stuff with polyester stuffing as you proceed.

Rnds 3-26: Sc in each sc around.

Note: This is 24 rnds at 12 sts each for a total of 288 sts worked in spiral if you like to count that way.

Rnd 27: (scdec over next 2 sts) six times total, sl st to first st made, ch 3 more, cut yarn leaving a long tail, use tail to sew any rem hole closed.

CONDIMENTS

Ketchup

Using D held double stranded and Size US H (5 mm) crochet hook, ch 23.

Row 1: (sc/hdc/sc) in the 2nd bb from hook, (3scdec [pull up a lp in each of the next 3 bb, yo and pull through all lps on hook] over next 3 bb, [sc/hdc/sc] in the next bb) five times total, sl st in last st, ch 3 more, cut yarn leaving tail for sewing.

Create Join Ch

Cut an 18" strand of D, fold it in half. Insert hook from the right side of the sts through the first sc made on Row 1. Lay the lp end of the strand of yarn over the hook and pull through the st, ch 3, pull end tail through last ch made and pull tightly to secure.

Mustard

Using E, rep Ketchup exactly.

Relish

Using F held double stranded and Size US H (5 mm) crochet hook, ch 21.

Rnd 1: Sl st in 2nd bb from hook, ch 2, sl st in 2nd bb from hook, sl st in next bb on ch, (ch 2, sl st in 2nd bb from hook, sl st in next 2 bb on ch, ch 2, sl st in 2nd bb from hook, sl st in next 3 bb on ch) three times total, ch 2, sl st in 2nd bb from hook, sl st in next 2 bb on ch, 3 sc in last ch, working in the rem lps of the beg ch up the next side, sl st in next st, (ch 3, sl st in 2nd and 3rd bb from hook, sl st in next 3 sts on ch, ch 2, sl st in 2nd bb from hook, sl st in next 2 sts on ch) three times total, ch 2, sl st in 2nd BB from hook, sl st in next st on ch, sl st to

center st on end, ch 3 more, cut yarn 8" long, pull through last ch made tightly to secure.

Follow Create Join Ch from Ketchup, to create join ch for Relish.

Diced Onions

Using G held double stranded and Size US H (5 mm) crochet hook, ch 21.

Rnd 1: Sl st in 2nd bb from hook, *ch 2, sl st in 2nd bb from hook, ch 3, sl st in 2nd bb from hook, sl st in next 4 bb on ch*, rep * -* three more times, 3 sc in same ch as last sl st made, working in the rem lps up the opposite side of the beg ch, rep * - * four times, ch 3, cut yarn leaving long tail for sewing.

FINISHING

Using the end tail from ch-5 end of the hot dog, sew the end of the hot dog inside the bun at the point where you began to sew the 2 bun halves tog.

Using the tail end from the opposite side of the hot dog and the tail end of one side of the mustard, knot them tog tightly as close to the end of each ch-3 as possible. Weave the tail end of each color back into its own piece. For example, weave C tail back down ch-3 and into hot dog and E tail down ch-3 and back into mustard. Join the ketchup to the mustard in the same way, then join the relish. Finally join the end of the diced onions with the ch-3 to the end of the relish. The other end of the diced onions has no ch-3. Weave in all ends. To assemble for play, this works best if you fold the hot dog in first and then "spiral" the toppings around the hot dog.

SLICEABLE
Watermelon

Take your crochet to a fun new level with this adorable watermelon that looks good enough to eat!

Half Double Crochet Spike stitch gives the outer skin of the melon it's realistic look, while working into the back bump of the beginning chains provides neat and tidy edging. A simple loop closure makes it easy to "slice" into the melon and put back together after playtime is done.

FINISHED SIZE
Closed watermelon measures approximately 7" tall x 7" wide x 11" long.

YARN
Worsted weight (#4 Medium).

Shown here: Red Heart Super Saver (100% acrylic; 364 yards/198 grams): Shocking Pink (A), White (B), Black (C), Spring Green (D), Medium Thyme (E), 1 skein each.

HOOK
Size US F (3.75 mm) crochet hook.

Adjust hook size as necessary to obtain correct gauge.

NOTIONS
Basic crochet tool kit.

Polyester stuffing.

GAUGE
Gauge not critical, but stitches should be *very* tight so it can be stuffed without distorting and the stitches have no holes.

NOTES
- Do not join or turn rnds unless instructed.

- Mark first stitch of each rnd as needed to keep track.

- During color changes, do not cut the previous colored yarn unless specified.

SPECIAL STITCHES
Half Double Crochet Spike Stitch (spikehdc): When indicated, work the hdc as you normally would but insert the hook in the top of the st 2 rnds below and then sk st on the current rnd to create a spiked look to your st.

INNER FLESH (MAKE 2)

Using A, ch 21.

Rnd 1: Sc in 2nd bb from hook (see "*How to Work in Back Bump of a Chain*" lesson), mark st just made, sc in next 18 bb, 3 sc in last bb, working in the rem lps up opposite side of beg ch (creating an oval shape), sc in next 18 sts, 2 sc in last ch. (42 sc)

Note: Be sure to count sts to confirm, once correct here and throughout, move the marker to the first st made in the next rnd.

Rnd 2: *Sc 2 in each of next 3 sc, sc in next 14 sc, 2 sc in each of next 3 sc, 3 sc in next sc, rep from * one more time. (58 sc)

Rnd 3: Sc 2 in each of next 4 sc, hdc in next 18, 2 sc in each of next 4 sc, 3 sc in next sc, 2 sc in each of next 4 sc, hdc in next 22 sc, 2 sc in each of next 4 sc, 3 in last sc, sl st to first st. (78 sts)

Rnd 4: Ch 1 (does not count as st here and throughout) hdc in same st as ch-1 and in each st around.

Rnds 5-6: Hdc in each st around.

Rnd 7: Hdc 2 in each of next 2 sts, hdc in next st, (2 hdc in next st, hdc in next) twice, 2 hdc in each of next 2 hdc, hdc in next 25 hdc, (2 hdc in next hdc, hdc in next hdc) nine times total, hdc in next 20 hdc, (2 hdc in next, hdc in next hdc) three times total, sl st to first st made. (96 sts)

Rnd 8: Ch 1, hdc in same st as ch-1 and each st around, sl st to first st made.

Rnd 9: Ch 1, hdc in same st as ch-1, hdc in next st, (2 hdc in next, 1 hdc in next) five times total, hdc in next 32, (2 hdc in next, hdc in next) ten times total, hdc in next 25, (2 hdc in next, 1 hdc in next) three times total, hdc in last st. (114 sts)

Rnd 10: Hdc in each st around, sl st to first st made, change to B, cut A.

Rnd 11: Ch 1, hdc in same st as ch-1 and each hdc around, sl st to first st made and cut yarn.

SEEDS

Using a double strand of C and tapestry needle, double st seeds onto flesh using photos as a guide so they are on the right side of the sts. It does not matter what the wrong side of the flesh looks like as it will be enclosed inside the toy when joining.

OUTER SKIN (MAKE 2)

Using E, ch 21.

Rnd 1: Sc in 2nd bb from hook, mark st just made, sc in next 18 bb, 3 sc in last bb, working in the rem lps up opposite side of beg ch (creating an oval shape), sc in next 18 chs, 2 sc in last ch. Be sure to count sts to confirm. Once correct count is confirmed, here and throughout, move the marker to the first st made in the next rnd. (42 sc)

Rnd 2: *2 sc in each of next 3 sc, sc in next 14 sc, 2 sc in each of next 3 sc, 3 sc in next sc, rep from *, one more time. (58 sc)

Rnd 3: 2 sc in each of next 4 sc, hdc in next 18 sc, 2 sc in each of next 4 sc, 3 sc in next sc, 2 sc in each of next 4 sc, hdc in next 22 sc, 2 sc in each of next 4 sc, 3 in last sc, sl st to first st while changing to D, and dropping E. Carry the dropped yarn on the wrong side of the sts as you work here and throughout the remainder of the piece. (78 sts)

Rnd 4: Ch 1 (does not count as st here and throughout) hdc in same st as ch-1, spikehdc (see Special Stitches) in next st, *hdc in next st, spikehdc in next st, rep from * around, sl st to first st while changing to E, drop D.

How to Work in Back Bump of a Chain

Working into the bb of your beg ch gives the start of your work a cleaner look, allows easier edging, and creates visual symmetry between the top and bottom of rnds.

First, create the beg ch as instructed in a normal fashion. Then, flip the ch over and find the "bumps" that run along the back of the ch (Figure 1). Instead of working in the standard lps of the ch, insert your hook under the bump and complete st as normal.

Fig. 1

Rnd 5: Ch 1, hdc same st as ch-1 and in each st around.

Rnd 6: Hdc in each st around.

Rnd 7: Hdc 2 in each of next 2 sts, hdc in next st, (2 hdc in next st, hdc in next) twice, 2 hdc in each of next 2 hdc, hdc in next 25 hdc, (2 hdc in next hdc, hdc in next hdc) nine times total, hdc in next 20 hdc, (2 hdc in next, hdc in next hdc) three times total, sl st to first st while changing to D, drop E. (96 sts)

Rnd 8: Ch 1, hdc in same st, spikehdc in next st, *hdc in next st, spikehdc in next st, rep from * around, sl st to first st while changing to E, drop D.

Rnd 9: Ch 1, 2 hdc in same st as ch-1, hdc in next st, (2 hdc in next, 1 hdc in next) five times total, hdc in next 32, (2 hdc in next, hdc in next) ten times total, hdc in next 25, (2 hdc in next, 1 hdc in next) three times total, hdc in last st. (115 hdc)

Rnd 10: Hdc each st around.

Rnd 11: Hdc in each st around, sl st to first st while changing to D, drop E.

Rnd 12: Ch 1, hdc in same st as ch-1, spikehdc in next st, *hdc in next st, spikehdc in next st, rep from * around until 3 sts rem, hdcdec over next 2 sts, spikehdc in last st, sl st to first st while changing to E, drop D. (114 sts)

Rnds 13-14: Ch 1, hdc in same st as ch-1 and in each hdc around, sl st to first st made.

Rnd 15: Ch 1, hdc in same st as ch-1 and in each hdc around, sl st to first st made while changing to D, drop E.

Rnd 16: Ch 1, hdc in same st as ch-1, spikehdc in next st, *hdc in next st, spikehdc in next st, rep from * around, sl st to first st made while changing to E, cut D.

Rnd 17: Ch 1, sc in same st as ch-1 and each st around, sl st to first st made, do not cut yarn, cont to join to Inner Flesh.

FINISHING
Join Rnd

First Half: Lay the Inner Flesh inside the Outer Skin so the pieces match and both wrong sides are touching. Keeping the lp on the hook from the last rnd of the Outer Skin, insert the hook into the same st on the Outer Skin first and then the matching st on the Inner Flesh, yo and pull up a lp, then sc through both the st on the Inner Flesh and Outer Skin to join them tog with the sc. Before doing final 10 sc, stuff lightly (be sure not to overstuff and bulge), sl st to first sc made, cut yarn.

Second Half: Rep exactly as for first half.

CLOSURE SYSTEM
Loop

With one half of the watermelon placed with the green side up, visually locate the center most st on one of the narrow ends of the oval (either end is fine). Working a double strand of E, join to that center st with a sl st, ch 8, sl st to the same st you joined to forming a lp. Cut yarn, weave ends into melon.

Stem

With the other half of the watermelon placed with the green side up, visually locate the center most st on one of the narrow ends of the oval (either end is fine for this). Working a double strand of E, join to that center st with a sl st, then ch 4, sc in the 2nd hump from hook and each rem hump. Cut yarn, weave the ends into the melon.

Hinge

Place the melon halves on top of each other, pink sides touching with the lp and stem on the same side. Wrap the ch-8 lp around the stem. Locate st closest to center on opposite end from the stem/lp combo. Using E, join w sl st through both thicknesses at the 4th st to the right of the center st, ch 1, sc in same st and in next 8 sts across to create hinge. Weave in any rem ends on watermelon.

To close, wrap ch-8 lp around stem.

BEE-UNIFIED
Mobile

Busy little bees are buzzing all around in this twist on the classic mobile! A soft and natural color pallet is sure to lull and enthrall your little ones, while the ultra-textured hive, organic branch, and thoughtful adornments make this heirloom-worthy décor item the utmost of lush and luxury.

FINISHED SIZE

Bees measure approximately 3.5" tall.

Hive measures approximately 7.5" tall.

Constructed mobile measures approximately 20" wide x 11" tall.

YARN

DK weight (#3 Light).

Shown here: Knit Picks CotLin (70% cotton, 30% linen; 123 yards/50 grams): Linen (A), Black (B), Canary (C), Sagebrush (D), Raindrop (E), Pennyroyal (F), Coffee (G), Thicket (H), Crème Brulee (I), Flamingo (J), White (K), Pink (L), 1 skein each.

HOOKS

Size US C (2.75 mm) crochet hook.
Size US F (3.75 mm) crochet hook.

Adjust hook size as necessary to obtain correct gauge.

NOTIONS

Basic crochet tool kit.
Polyester stuffing.
(1) 3" metal ring.

Wired jute twine and craft twig about 20" long with waves or bends for visual interest if possible. You can find this in the floral section of your craft store. If wired jute twine is unavailable, regular twine will work as well.

Small wire cutters if using wired twine, glue sticks and glue gun if using regular twine.

5" diameter circle of a stiff material to support the base of the hive. Some options are sturdy cardboard, doubled plastic canvas, or a circle cut from a plastic folder available in the office section of your store.

GAUGE

Gauge is not critical, although sts should be quite tight so objects hold shape when stuffed and stated yarn amounts are used.

NOTES

- I recommend using cotton yarn for this project as it provides great stitch definition and crisper details.

- Do not turn or join rnds unless specifically instructed.

- During color changes, DO NOT cut the previous colored yarn unless specified. Instead carry the dropped yarn inside the project as you work.

- Going against standards, the beehive in this project has the wrong side of the sts on the outside of the hive and visible. This creates a more rustic appearance more in line with a real beehive.

SPECIAL STITCHES

Invisible Single Crochet Decrease (invscdec): Do not yo, insert your hook under the flo of the next st, do not yo, insert your hook though flo of the next st. (Shown in image) Yo and pull through the 2 front lps at once (2 lps on the hook). Yo and pull through the 2 lps on the hook to complete. This method allows a near invisible dec with no holes and is the preferred method for toys and amigurumi when tight stitching and dec are optimal.

Cluster Stitch (CL): (sc, dc, sc) all in the same st indicated.

BEES (MAKE 5 TOTAL)

Body and Head

Using B and Size US C (2.75 mm) crochet hook, make magic ring. (See Magic Ring on page 17).

Rnd 1: Ch 1, 6 sc in ring, pull tail tightly to close ring. (6 sc)

Rnd 2: Sc 2 in each sc around, sl st to first st while changing to C, drop B. Make sure the right side of the sts are on the outside and your hook is pointing into the center of the circle as you work. (12 sc)

Rnd 3: Ch 1, sc in same sc as ch-1, 2 sc in next sc, *sc in next sc, 2 sc in next sc, rep from *, four more times, sl st to first sc made. (18 sc)

Rnd 4: Ch 1, sc in same sc as ch-1, sc in next sc, 2 sc in next sc, *sc in next 2 sc, 2 sc in next sc, rep from *, four more times, sl st to first sc while changing to B, drop C. (24 sc)

Rnd 5: Ch 1, sc same sc as ch-1 and in each sc around, sl st to first sc made.

Rnd 6: Ch 1, sc in same sc as ch-1 and in each sc around, sl st to first sc while changing to C, drop B.

Rnd 7: Ch 1, sc in same sc as ch-1 and in each sc around, sl st to first sc made.

Rnd 8: Ch 1, sc in same sc and in each sc around, sl st to first sc while changing to B, drop C.

Rnd 9: Ch 1, sc in same sc as ch-1 and next sc, invscdec (see Special Stitches) next 2 sc tog, *sc in next 2 sc, invscdec next 2 sc tog, rep from *, four more times, sl st to first sc made. (18 sts)

Rnd 10: Ch 1, sc same st and in each st around, sl st to first sc made while changing to C, drop B.

Rnd 11: Ch 1, sc in same st as ch-1, invscdec next 2 sc tog, *sc in next sc, invscdec next 2 sc tog, rep from *, 4 more times, sl st to first sc made. (12 sc)

Note: Begin to stuff here and cont through until end of piece.

Rnd 12: Ch 1, sc in same st and in each st around, sl st to first sc while changing to B, cut C.

Rnd 13: Ch 1, sc in same st as ch-1 and in each st around, sl st to first sc made.

Rnd 14: Ch 1, sc in same sc and in each sc around, sl st to first sc made.

Rnd 15: Ch 1, sc in same sc, 2 sc in next sc, *sc in next sc, 2 sc in next sc, rep from *, four more times. (18 sc)

Rnds 16-18: Working in spiral and not joining rnds, sc in each sc around.

Rnd 19: (sc in next sc, invscdec next 2 sc tog) 6 times. (12 sts)

Rnd 20: (invscdec next 2 sc tog) 6 times, sl st to first st made, cut yarn. Use end tail to sew any rem hole closed. (6 sts)

Face

Make one each using G, H, I, J, and L.

Using Size US C (2.75 mm) crochet hook, make magic ring.

Rnd 1: Ch 1, 5 sc in ring, pull end to close ring. (5 sc)

Rnd 2: Sc 2 in each sc around, sl st to first sc made, tie off, leaving long tail for sewing later. (10 sc)

Wings

Using K and Size US F (3.75 mm) crochet hook, ch 2.

Row 1: Sc 2 in 2nd ch from hook, ch 1, turn.

Row 2: Sc 2 in each sc across, ch 1, turn. (4 sc)

Rows 3-4: Sc in each sc across, ch 1, turn.

Row 5: (scdec next 2 sc tog) 2 times, ch 1, turn. (2 sc)

Row 6: Scdec next 2 sc tog, ch 1, turn. (1 sc)

Row 7: Sc 2 in sc, ch 1, turn. (2 sc)

Row 8: Sc 2 in each sc across, ch 1 to end, turn. (4 sc)

Rows 9-10: Sc in each sc across, ch 1, turn.

Row 11: (scdec next 2 sc tog) 2 times, ch 1, turn. (2 sc)

Row 12: Scdec next 2 sc tog, ch 1, cut yarn leaving long tail for sewing. (1 sc)

Antenna

Cut an 18" piece C. Insert Size US C (2.75 mm) crochet hook around post of st on top of head at position where you want the antenna to be, with the suggested position being near Rnd 21 of bee head. Fold the length of yarn in half, place lp end on hook and pull through the st on the body, using both thicknesses of the yarn as one, ch 4. Then, cut yarn and pull tail end through last ch made. Tie an overhand knot as close to final ch made and cut near knot. Make two antenna on each bee. Rep for all five bees.

Assembly

Sew one face to each bee on black (B) Rnds 15-18 of bee body. Make sure any seam from color changes on the body is positioned on the center back.

Using the long end tail from the wings, weave it across the wing so it is in the 1sc center of them. Sew to Rnd 11 of the bee body in center back opposite the face on top of the seam to camouflage any color changes even further.

HIVE

Main Hive

Using A and Size US F (3.75 mm) crochet hook, make magic ring.

Note: As you begin, mark the first sc of each CL around. This will help you identify them for placement on subsequent rnds. As you become familiar with the placement, you can discontinue marking them.

Rnd 1: Ch 1, 9 sc in ring, pull end tail to close ring. (9 sc)

Rnd 2: Sc 2 in each sc around, sl st to first st made. (18 sc)

Rnd 3: Ch 1, CL (see Special Stitches) in same st as ch-1, sk next 2 sts, (CL in next st, sk next 2 sts) five times total, sl st to first sc made. (6 CL)

Rnd 4: Ch 1, CL in same sc as ch-1, sk the sts in bet, CL is first sc of each CL made around, sl st to first sc made.

Rnd 5: Ch 1, 2 CL in same st as ch-1, sk the sts in bet, 2 CL in first sc of each CL around, sl st to first sc made. (12 CL)

Rnd 6: Ch 1, CL in same st as ch-1, sk the sts in bet, CL in first sc of each CL around, sl st to first sc made while changing to C, drop A.

Rnd 7: Ch 1, hdc in same st as ch-1, 2 hdc in next dc, hdc in next sc, *hdc in next sc, 2 hdc in next dc, hdc in next sc, rep from *, 10 more times, sl st to first hdc while changing to A, drop C. (48 hdc)

Rnd 8: Ch 1, CL in same st as ch-1, sk next 2 hdc, *CL in next hdc, sk next 2 hdc, rep from*, 14 more times, sl st to first sc made. (16 CL)

Rnd 9: Ch 1, CL in same st as ch-1 and CL in first sc of each CL around, sl st to first sc made.

Rnd 10: Ch 1, 2 CL in same st as ch-1 and 2 CL in first sc of each CL around, sl st to first sc made. (32 CL)

Rnd 11: Ch 1, CL in same st as ch-1 and CL in first sc of each CL around, sl st to first sc while changing to C, drop A.

Rnd 12: Ch 1, CL in same st as ch-1 and CL in first sc of each CL around, sl st to first sc while changing to A, drop C.

Rnd 13: Ch 1, CL in same st as ch-1, and in first sc of each CL around, sl st to first sc made.

Rnds 14-15: Ch 1, CL in same st as ch-1 and in first sc of each CL around, sl st to first sc made.

Rnd 16: Ch 1, CL in same st as ch-1 and in first sc of each CL around, sl st to first sc made, sl st to first st while changing to C, drop A.

Rnd 17: Ch 1, CL in same st as ch-1 and in first sc of each CL around, sl st to first sc while changing to A, drop C.

Rnds 18-22: Ch 1, CL in same st as ch-1 and in first sc of each CL around, sl st to first sc made.

Rnd 23: Ch 1, CL in same st as ch-1 and in first sc of each CL around, sl st to first sc while changing to C, drop A.

Rnd 24: Ch 1, CL in same st as ch-1 and in first sc of each CL around, sl st to first sc made.

Rnd 25: Ch 1, CL in same st as ch-1 and in first sc of each CL around, sl st to first sc while changing to A, drop C.

Rnd 26: Ch 1, CL in same st as ch-1 and in first sc of each CL around, sl st to first sc made.

Rnd 27-31: Ch 1, CL in same st as ch-1 and in first sc of each CL around, sl st to first sc made.

Rnd 32: Ch 1, CL in same st as ch-1 and in first sc of each CL around, sl st to first sc while changing to C, drop A.

Rnds 33-34: Ch 1, CL in same st as ch-1 and in first sc of each CL around.

Rnd 35: Ch 1, CL in same st as ch-1 and in first sc of each CL around, sl st to first sc while changing to A, cut C.

Rnd 36: Ch 1, sc in same st as ch-1, sc in next 91 sts, (invscdec next 2 sts tog) twice, sl st to first st made, cut yarn. (94 sts)

Base of Hive

Using A and Size US F (3.75 mm) crochet hook, make magic ring.

Rnd 1: Ch 1 (does not count as st here and throughout), 10 hdc. (10 hdc)

Rnd 2: Hdc 2 in each st around. (20 hdc)

Rnd 3: (hdc in next st, 2 hdc in next st) ten times total. (30 hdc)

Rnd 4: (hdc in next 4 sts, 2 hdc in next st) six times total. (36 hdc)

Rnd 5: (hdc in next 5 sts, 2 hdc in next st) six times total. (42 hdc)

Rnd 6: (hdc in next 5 sts, 2 hdc in next st) seven times total. (49 hdc)

Rnd 7: (hdc in next 6 sts, 2 hdc in next st) seven times total. (56 hdc)

Rnd 8: (hdc in next 7 sts, 2 hdc in next st) seven times total. (63 hdc)

Rnd 9: (hdc in next 6 sts, 2 hdc in next st) nine times total. (72 hdc)

Rnd 10: (sc in next 2 sts, 2 sc in next st) 22 times total, sc in last 6 sts, sl st to first st made, leave long tail for sewing. (94 sc)

Hive Door

Using B and Size US F (3.75 mm) crochet hook, ch 11.

Row 1: Sc in 2nd ch from hook and each rem ch, ch 1, turn. (10 sc)

Row 2: Sc in each sc across, ch 1, turn.

Row 3: Scdec first 2 sc tog, sc in next 6 sc, scdec last 2 sc tog, ch 1, turn. (8 sc)

Row 4: Sc in each sc across, ch 1, turn.

Row 5: Scdec first 2 sc tog, sc in next 4 sc, scdec last 2 sc tog, ch 1, turn. (6 sc)

Rows 6-7: Sc in each sc across, ch 1, turn.

Row 8: Scdec first 2 sc tog, sc in next 2 sc, scdec last 2 sc tog, ch 1, turn. (4 sc)

Row 9: Sc in each sc across, ch 1, turn.

Row 10: Sc in first st, scdec over next 2 sts, sc in last st, do not cut yarn, cont to Edge Rnd. (3 sc)

Edge Rnd: Do not turn, ch 1, sc around post of st at each end of each of the 9 rows down the first long side, 3 sc in first st along bottom, sc in next 8 sts, 3 sc in last st, sc around post of each st at end of each of the 9 rows up the 2nd long side, 3 sc in first st along top (Row 9), sc in next, 3 sc in last, sl st to first sc made, cut yarn leaving long tail for sewing.

Align the base on the open end of the hive. There are 94 sts in the final rnd of each part. Using the long tail from the end of the base, begin sewing the base on the open end of the hive matching st for st. Stop when you are a little over halfway around the base. Slide the 5" diameter circle you have prepared and stuff the hive. Complete sewing the base onto the hive and weave in any ends to this point. Using the tail end from the hive door, sew it in place aligned with the bottom edge of the hive.

FLOWER COMBO

Leaf (Make 3)

Using D and Size US F (3.75 mm) crochet hook, ch 12.

Rnd 1: Sc in 2nd ch from hook and next 2 chs, hdc in next 2 chs, dc in next 3 chs, tr in next 2 chs, 9 tr in last ch, working in free lps on opposite side of ch, tr in next 2 chs, dc in next 3 chs, hdc in next 2 chs, sc in last 2 chs, sl st to first sc made, tie off.

Flower

Make 3 of each color using E, F, and L.

Using Size US F (3.75 mm) crochet hook, make magic ring.

Rnd 1: Ch 1, 10 sc in ring, sl st to first sc made, pull end to close ring. (10 sc)

Rnd 2: Ch 1, (sc, hdc, 2 dc, hdc, sc) in same sc as sl st, sc in next sc, *(sc, hdc, 2 dc, hdc, sc) in next sc, sc in next sc, rep from *, 3 more times, sl st to first sc made, cut yarn leaving long tail for sewing. (5 petals)

Sew one flower on the wider end of each leaf for three leaf/flower combinations total.

FINISHING

Wrap the metal wring tightly in the wired twine, snip wire leaving a 14" tail. If using regular twine, wrap the entire ring tightly, laying a very small amount of hot glue on the ring as you progress, then wrapping the twine over that to secure it in place. Trim to 14" as well.

Cut five lengths of the twine that are 18" long. For wired twine, insert one end through the sts of one bee to the rear of the head. Mine stayed inserted quite well, but secure with the tiniest dab of glue if you feel it necessary. For regular twine, use a tapestry needle and weave one end into the rear of the head and through the body to secure. Attach a 12" piece of twine to the top center of the hive in the same manner.

If using wired twine, wrap the free end of the twine from the hive around the center of the branch about three times, then trim the wire flush. In the same manner, space the bees out as desired (I did two left of the hive and three right) and wrap the twine around the branch varying the lengths they hang. Then, snip wire and trim flush. If using regular twine, arrange in the same manner but wrap the twine around and then knot securely a few times, then trim.

Using the tail end from wrapping the metal ring, attach the ring to the top of the branch above the center of the hive. Wrap in an "X" shape around multiple times to secure. Finally, using hot glue or the tail ends, glue or sew the three flower/leaf combos on the branch, two on either end of the branch and one at the base of the ring. Weave in any rem ends. Be sure if using around a child, it is secure and out of reach, the piece is not designed to be a toy and is strictly a décor item.

ROLL-AWAY
Kitchen Playmat

Big on imagination and small on space, your little one can cook meals and do dishes with bubbly soap on this adorable playmat. To store, simply roll up and secure with the tie strands. An absolute treasure of a toy!

FINISHED SIZE
Assembled mat measures approximately 23" wide x 19" tall.

YARN
Worsted weight (#4 Medium).

Shown here: Red Heart Super Saver (100% acrylic; 364 yards/198 grams): Black (A), Light Grey (B), Charcoal (C), Cherry Red (D), White (E), Turqua (F), Blue (G), Hot Red (H), Bright Yellow (I), Pretty in Pink (J), Guava (K), 1 skein each.

Caron Simply Soft (100% acrylic; 315 yards/ 170 grams): Party Silver Sparkle (L), Off White (M), 1 skein each.

HOOKS
Size US H (5mm) crochet hook.

Size US K (6.5mm) crochet hook.

Adjust hook size as necessary to obtain correct gauge.

NOTIONS
Basic crochet tool kit.

GAUGE
Rnds 1-6 of burner = 4" in diameter.

NOTES
- All parts made single strand unless noted as doubled.

- Do not turn or join rnds unless instructed. Mark rnds with st marker as needed.

- During color changes, do not cut the previous colored yarn unless specified.

- To assemble, you may either sew or use hot glue to assemble (yes, it does work!). If you choose hot glue, you will need glue gun and glue sticks. (I prefer Gorilla Glue brand available at my local box-store craft section).

BURNERS (MAKE 4)

Using A and Size US H (5 mm) crochet hook, make a magic ring. (See Magic Ring on page 17).

Rnd 1: Ch 1, sc 8 in ring. (8 sc)

Rnd 2: Sc 2 in each sc around. (16 sc)

Rnd 3: (sc in next sc, 2 sc in next sc) eight times total. (24 sc)

Rnd 4: (sc in next 2 sc, 2 sc in next sc) eight times total. (32 sc)

Rnd 5: (sc in next 3 sc, 2 sc in next sc) eight times total. (40 sc)

Rnd 6: (sc in next 4 sc, 2 sc in next sc) eight times total, sl st to next st, cut yarn. (48 sc)

GAUGE CHECK: The piece should measure about 4" in diameter now.

Rnd 7: Join B with a sl st in any sc around, ch 1, sc in same st and next 4 sts, 2 sc in next st, *sc in next 5 sc, 2 sc in next sc, rep from * six more times. (56 sc)

Rnd 8: Ch 1, revsc (see Reverse Single Crochet on page 15) in each st around, sl st to first st made, cut yarn leaving a long tail to sew to mat later.

Burner Coil

Holding D double stranded, insert hook from front to back in st near the center of the burner, lp yarn over the end of the hook from the back side, pull lp through the black to the front. You will work the rest of burner-coil stitches using this method of surface crochet.

Cont working in spiral motion by inserting the hook into the next st in rnd of burner below (this is partially artistic, just work in a concentric circle) and pull D through the burner and the lps on the front in red, thereby creating a sl st.

Work Burner Coil out until you have about 4 rnds, then cut D and pull the ends through to the reverse of the work.

KNOBS (MAKE 4)
Bottom

Using C and Size US H (5 mm) crochet hook, make magic ring.

Rnd 1: Ch 1, 8 sc in the ring. (8 sc)

Rnd 2: Sc 2 in each sc around. (16 sc)

Rnd 3: (sc in next sc, 2 sc in next sc) eight times total, sl st to first st made. (24 sc)

Rnd 4: Ch 1 revsc in each sc around, sl st to first st made, cut yarn.

Top

Using B, make magic ring.

Rnd 1: Ch 1, 8 sc in ring. (8 sc)

Rnd 2: Sc 2 in each sc around, sl st to next sc, cut yarn leaving long tail to sew to bottom. (16 sc)

Using the end tail from the top part, sew it to the center middle of the bottom part.

Using the photo as a guide, use separate strands of A held doubled stranded to sew a line to represent the line to "turn on the burner." I went twice around from the edge of the top through the center.

SINK
Water

Using F and Size US H (5 mm) crochet hook, ch 26.

Row 1: Hdc in 2nd ch from hook (sk ch and turning ch-1 do not count as a st here and throughout the sink), and in each rem ch across. (25 hdc)

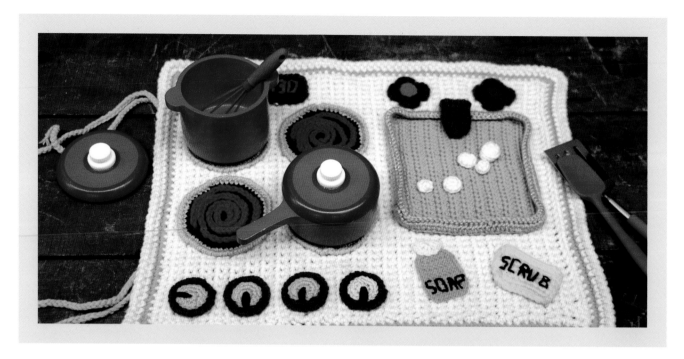

Rows 2-18: Ch 1, turn, hdc in each st across, do not cut yarn, cont to Edge Rnd.

Edge Rnd: Ch 1, do not turn, work 3 sc sp evenly in the end of each 2 rows of hdc (an hdc is slightly bigger than an sc, so to avoid puckering the work, you will need 3 sc for each 2 rows), sc in each st and make 3 sc in each corner around the perimeter of the piece, once around, sl st to first sc made, then cut yarn.

Sink Rim

Holding a strand each of B and L together, join in any st around the perimeter of the water just completed.

Rnd 1: Ch 1, sc in each st around, make 3 sc in each corner, sl st to the flo of the first sc made.

Rnd 2: Ch 1, hdcflo in each st around, working 3 hdcflo in each corner st, sl st to first hdcflo made.

Rnd 3: Ch 1, sl st blo in each st around (no need to do 3 in corners, just 1), sl st to firstt sl st made, cut yarn.

Small Soap Bubbles (Make 2)

Note: *Working this small in the rnd tends to make the work flip inside out. Just turn it so the right side of the sts are facing out before sewing to water.*

Using E and Size US H (5 mm) crochet hook, make magic ring.

Rnd 1: Sc 6 in ring. (6 sc)

Rnd 2: Sc in each sc around, sl st to next st, cut yarn leaving long tail to sew to sink water.

Medium Soap Bubbles (Make 2)

Using E and Size US H (5 mm) crochet hook, make magic ring, ch 1.

Rnd 1: Sc 8 in ring. (8 sc)

Rnd 2: Sc in each sc around, sl st to next st, cut yarn leaving long tail to sew to sink water.

Large Soap Bubble (Make 1)

Using E and Size US H (5 mm) crochet hook, make magic ring, ch 1.

Rnd 1: Sc 10 in ring. (10 sc)

Rnd 2: Sc in each sc around.

Rnd 3: Scblo in each st around, sl st to first st made, cut yarn leaving long tail to sew to sink water.

Spout

Using C held double stranded and Size US H (5 mm) crochet hook, ch 4.

Row 1: Sc in 2nd ch from hook and next 2 chs. (3 sc)

Rows 2-10: Ch 1, turn, sc in each st across.

Row 11: Ch 1, turn, sc dec over first 2 sc, sc in last sc. (2 sts)

Row 12: Ch 1, turn, sc dec over the 2 sts, do not cut yarn, cont to Edge Rnd. (1 st)

Edge Rnd: Do not turn, ch 1, sc in the end of each row up the long side, make 3 sc in the first st in the rem free lp of Row 1, sc in next sc, 3 sc in last sc, sc in the end of each row down the 2nd long side, making 2 sc in the last row end instead of one, sl st to first sc made, cut yarn leaving a long tail to sew to sink.

Spout Accent

Using C held double stranded and Size US H (5 mm) crochet hook, make magic ring.

Rnd 1: Ch 1, 7 sc in ring, sl st to first sc made, cut yarn leaving long tail to sew to faucet later.

Handles (Make 2)

Using C held double stranded and Size US H (5 mm) crochet hook, make magic ring.

Rnd 1: Ch 1, sc 8 in ring. (8 sc)

Rnd 2: Sc 2 in each sc around, sl st to first sc made. (16 sc)

Rnd 3: Ch 1 (counts as sl st), 2 hdc in each of next 2 sts, sl st in next st, *sl st in next st, 2 hdc in each of next 2 sts, sl st in next st, rep from * two more times, sl st to first ch-1 made, cut yarn leaving long tail to sew to mat later.

Temperature Dots

Make one temperature dot in each color using G and H.

Using Size US H (5 mm) crochet hook, make magic ring.

Rnd 1: Ch 1, 8 sc in ring, sl st to first sc made, cut yarn leaving long tail to sew to handles.

DISH SCRUBBY

Using I held double stranded and Size US H (5 mm) crochet hook, ch 9.

Row 1: Sc in 2nd ch from hook and each rem ch across. (8 sc)

Rows 2-5: Ch 1, turn, sc in each st across, do not cut yarn, cont to Edge Rnd.

Edge Rnd: Ch 1, do not turn, sc in each st and end of row around perimeter of scrubby working 3 sc in each corner, sl st to first sc made, cut yarn leaving long tail to sew to mat later.

With a separate strand of A and tapestry needle, sew the word "SCRUB" onto the scrubby. I know stitching words makes people nervous sometimes, but it does not have to be perfect.

SOAP BOTTLE

Using J and Size US H (5 mm) crochet hook, ch 7.

Row 1: Sc in 2nd ch from hook and each rem ch across. (6 sc)

Rows 2-8: Ch 1, turn, sc in each st across.

Row 9: Ch 1, turn, sc dec over first 2 sts, sc in next 2 sts, sc dec over last 2 sts. (4 sc)

Row 10: Ch 1, turn, sc in first sc, sc dec over next 2 sts, sc in last sc, do not cut yarn, cont to Edge Rnd. (3 sc)

Edge Rnd: Ch 1, do not turn, sc in end of each row down the first long side, make 3 sc in first st along bottom edge, sc in each st across until 1 st remains, make 3 sc in last st, sc in end of each row up 2nd long side, make 2 sc in the end of the last row instead of 1, sl st to first sc made, cut yarn leaving long tail to sew soap to sink later.

Soap Bottle Lid

Using M and Size US H (5 mm) crochet hook, make magic ring.

Row 1: Ch 1, make 4 sc in ring. (4 sc)

Row 2: Ch 1, turn, 2 sc in first sc, sc in next 2 sc, 2 sc in last sc, do not cut yarn, cont along bottom edge, evenly sp 4 sc, then sl st to first st made, cut yarn leaving long tail to sew to soap bottle.

With a strand of A, and starting right inside the Edge Rnd, sew the word "SOAP" on the bottle.

CLOCK

With A held double stranded and Size US H (5 mm) crochet hook, ch 9.

Row 1: Sc in 2nd ch from hook and each rem ch across. (8 sc)

Rows 2-4: Ch 1, turn, sc in each st across, do not cut yarn, cont to Edge Rnd.

Edge Rnd

Rnd 1: Ch 1, do not turn, sc in each st and row end around the perimeter of the piece working 3 sc in each corner, sl st to first sc made, cut yarn.

Rnd 2: Holding C double stranded, join with a sl st in any st around on Rnd 1, ch 1, sl st in next st, ch 1, (sl st, ch 1) in every st around, sl st to first sl st made, cut yarn.

Using a separate strand of D and tapestry needle, sew the time of your choice onto the clock face.

MAIN MAT

Using E held double stranded and Size US K (6.5 mm) crochet hook, ch 42.

Row 1: Sc in 2nd ch from hook and in each rem ch across. (41 sc)

Rows 2-54: Ch 1, turn, sc in each st across, do not cut yarn, cont to Edge Rnd.

Edge Rnd

Rnd 1: Ch 1, sc in each st and end of row around the perimeter of the mat, make 3 sc in each corner, when around, sl st to first sc made, cut yarn.

Rnd 2: Holding the yarn double stranded, join K in the 2nd sc of any 3 sc corner with a sl st, ch 1, 3 sc in same st, sc in each st around, working 3 sc in each corner st, sl st to first sc made, cut yarn.

Rnd 3: Holding the yarn double stranded, join E in the 2nd sc any 3sc corner with a sl st, ch 1, 3 sc in same st, sc in each st around, working 3 sc in each corner st, sl st to first sc made.

Rnd 4: Ch 1, (sl st, ch 1) in every st around, meaning ch-1 bet every sl st, once around sl st to first sl st made, cut yarn.

TIE STRANDS (MAKE 2)

Using K held double stranded and Size US H (5 mm) crochet hook, ch 90, pull end through tightly to secure. Trim both ends evenly at about ½".

Using a separate strand of K, sew the middle of each strand to the reverse side of the mat evenly spaced and on the green rnd of the main mat on the same side. To store, roll up mat and tie ends tog to secure.

FINISHING
Sewn Assembly Option

Notes: *Use photos as a guide throughout. Instead of stitching all the way from front to back on the mat, just catch the top of the strands of the sts on the mat so the sewing does not show on the reverse side.*

With right side of the Edge Rnd on the mat facing up, pin all in place to be sure you have everything where you want it before you make it permanent with sewing.

Weave in all ends on the burners, except for long B end tail. Sew the four burners evenly spaced as shown on the left side of the mat.

Weave in all ends on knobs, except for the long light gray tail. Sew the four knobs below and evenly spaced below the burners.

Sew the soap bottle lid to the soap bottle top with the wider end facing up. Weave in all ends on the soap and scrubby except for long end tail of each. Sew them to the mat to the right of the knobs, slightly offset from horizontal (see photo for angle). Weave in all ends.

Sew the sink to the mat above the soap and scrubby. You may need to use a separate strand of L to secure all the way around. Using a separate strand of F, randomly tack the water section down in a few spots so it doesn't lift from the mat. Sew the bubbles into the sink, a small/medium/large in a cl, then a small/medium separate off to the bottom left. Weave in all ends on these.

Sew one temperature dot on the top of each sink handle. Sew the spout accent to the narrow tip of the spout. Sew the spout overlapping the top middle of the sink. I left the middle of it free and only sewed each end down. Sew the hot handle to the left and the cold handle to the right. Weave in all ends.

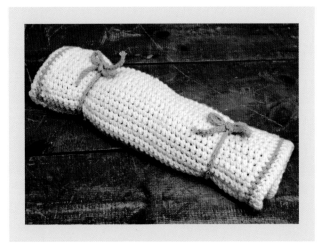

Sew the clock centered above the burners.

Weave in any rem ends.

Glued Assembly Option

Note: *The key is to take your time here. The hot glue is a one-shot deal. Once it is adhered it is nearly impossible to remove, hence why I really feel it works. It can also be washed by hand or on gentle if needed! Do not let this scare you, it really is not hard, just don't rush it. When I add the glue to the back, I take care to make sure a little touch of glue covers the knotted ends to fully secure them.*

Knot all ends tog to a near one on the back of each piece, trim to about ¼" long, then place all the items on the mat where you want them to be.

Glue all of the small pieces such as the knobs and handles and temperature dots. When lifting the glue gun from the pieces, swirl the tip around and pull away do you don't get the long wisp that you normally get.

Glue the larger pieces in sections. For example, for the burners, begin by adding glue to the top edge, press that into position. Once it dries a little, lift the piece up and glue and secure the next little section down. Rep until the whole piece is adhered. The sink needs to be done in the same manner.

ACKNOWLEDGMENTS

This book is dedicated to the beautiful souls that crave a vivid passionate tactile life. By night, I urge you stand under the brightest moon; arms outstretched, head back, bare feet anchored on the cool firm earth, breathing in the pulsating energy of the universe. By day, go and gather the softest yarns and brightest fibers to weave your magical soul into and share them with your fellow spirits. Clothe your babies, warm your loved ones, and color your outside to reflect your prismatic inner self. My gracious Maker, my sweetest babies, my family, and my friends are the reason I live and breathe. My creations are my way to let them hold my love in their hands and I hope this book empowers you to do the same.

Much love and yarn,
Stephanie

ABOUT THE AUTHOR

Owner and sole creator at Crochetverse, Stephanie Pokorny is a talented crochet designer with a fresh, out-of-the-box original style. Her children are her driving force and her impressive crochet costumes for them were featured in *Ripley's Believe It or Not* in 2019, and she has also received national attention from Good Morning America, *People Magazine*, *National Geographic Kids*, BoredPanda.com, MyModernMet.com, Mashable.com, and Insider.com, as well as an appearance on *The Kelly Clarkson Show*. Breathing new life into the art and craft of crochet, Stephanie is a one-of-a-kind creator with an unrivaled attention to detail, color, texture, and whimsy. You can find her work on her website (www.crochetverse.com), her social media channels (@crochetverse), or on Raverly (www.ravelry.com/designers/stephanie-pokorny).

Index